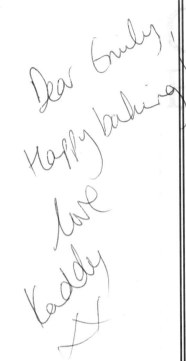

Dear Emily!
Happy baking
love
Kaddy
X

THE WESTLANDS SCHOOL
A FOUNDATION SCHOOL
SITTINGBOURNE

PRESENTED TO

EMILY KILLICK

7MMC

The Westlands School Prize

for

Effort

HEADTEACHER

22/10/2003

Date

the COMPLETE Book of Baking

NEW HOLLAND

This edition published in 2001 by
New Holland Publishers (UK) Ltd
London • Cape Town • Sydney • Auckland

24 Nutford Place
London W1H 5DQ
United Kingdom

80 McKenzie Street
Cape Town 8001
South Africa

Level 1, Unit 4, 14 Aquatic Drive
Frenchs Forest, NSW 2086
Australia

Unit 1A, 218 Lake Road
Northcote, Auckland
New Zealand

ISBN 1 85974 738 8

Editors: Alison Leach and Elizabeth Frost
Designer: Rob House
Indexer: Sandie Vahl
Cover design: Rob House
Illustrator: Royston Lamond

Copy compiled by: Heilie Voges
Recipes tested at different altitudes by: Luiza Rigutto and Marlene van Staden
Photographer: Willie van Heerden
Styling: Heilie Voges and Myrna Klerck
Food preparation: Heilie Voges Myrna Klerck and Frieda Minnaar

Printed and bound in Malaysia by Times Offset (M) Sdn. Bhd.

CONTENTS

Introduction

INTRODUCTION

ALL THE RECIPES INCLUDED IN THIS BOOK HAVE BEEN TESTED USING VARIOUS TYPES OF FLOUR TO ENSURE BEST RESULTS AND FRESHNESS. THIS BOOK OF BAKING IS INTENDED FOR EVERYDAY USE AND THEREFORE INCLUDES SIMPLE AND ECONOMICAL RECIPES WITHIN THE REACH OF EVERYONE. EXPERIENCED AND INEXPERIENCED COOK ALIKE WILL BE ABLE TO ACHIEVE SUCCESS.

WHEAT

Wheat is one of the world's most important sources of food and is widely cultivated in all types of climates. It is relied upon as a staple food by a large part of the world's population.

The nutrients found in wheat are carbohydrates (starch), proteins, lipids, minerals and vitamins. These are stored in the wheat kernel, which is comprised of the following:

● Bran, the outer shell, which needs to be removed to produce pure flour. It contains a high proportion of roughage, is rich in minerals and plays a role in aiding digestion and preventing constipation.

● Endosperm is the usable inner part of the kernel. It is separated from the bran and crushed into a powder to form flour. An important source of starch, it provides warmth and energy.

● Germ, which is the beginning of the new wheat plant, is normally removed as its fat content has adverse effects on the flour-making process. The fat limits the keeping quality of flour – a good reason for storing wheat germ in the refrigerator.

The milling process

The raw wheat is conveyed to separators, which remove the straws, sticks and unwanted seeds so that only pure wheat passes on to be washed. Once washed, the wheat is whisked dry in a type of spin-drier and transported to storage bins.

Once blended, the wheat is ready to be milled and is conveyed to roller mills. After the wheat has passed through the first roller mill – this is known as the first break – it emerges as crushed wheat. When the wheat has moved through various breaking and reducing systems, it is sifted. This separates particles of different sizes, which are then passed on to the purifiers. These grade the mixture according to particle size and purity. The various products are then weighed and packed. The wheat remains untouched by human hand throughout the entire milling process.

TYPES OF FLOUR

To obtain the best use out of this book it is important to get to know some of the different flours that are available. Whichever type of flour you use for baking, remember that the moisture content of freshly packaged flour will be correct and results will probably be more reliable.

In the United Kingdom plain white flour is the most widely used, all-purpose kind. For this reason, it has been specified in many of the recipes. It can, however, be replaced by soft flour, known in some countries as cake flour. Soft flour has only become generally available in the United Kingdom fairly recently, so may not be familiar to you. Many manufacturers provide helpful hints on how to use it.

Soft flour

This is made from the purest, whitest part of the wheat, which is ground down very finely and then sifted through fine nylon sieves. It is of a very high standard, has a low protein content, which helps to give a melt-in-the-mouth texture to baked items.

The protein found in this and other flour is called gluten. It is the gluten in the flour that holds the mixture together.

Soft flour is suitable for many recipes, such as sponge cakes, special breads, pastry and biscuits. It can be stored for 2–3 months under ideal conditions, and up to 1 year in a refrigerator or freezer.

Self-raising flour

This is soft flour to which a raising agent has been added in order to give lightness to the baked product. It is used for quick-mix and baked products such as scones, waffles, cakes and some kinds of biscuit. Once the packet has been opened, it should be stored in an airtight container so that the raising agent remains fresh and active.

If self-raising flour is required and none is available, add 5 ml (1 tsp) baking powder to every 150 g (5 oz) soft flour. Sift together before using.

For wholemeal self-raising flour, add 5 ml (1 tsp) baking powder to every 150 g (5 oz) plain wholemeal flour. Sift the ingredients together several times before using.

Store self-raising flour for 2–3 months under ideal conditions, and for up to 1 year in a refrigerator or freezer.

White bread flour

This is a pure wheaten product which is used by bakeries to produce white bread. It is also known as strong flour.

It can be used for making loaf-type cakes, fruit cakes, pizza doughs, rusks and as a thickening agent in gravies and stews.

White bread flour can be stored for 2–3 months under ideal conditions, and for 1 year in a refrigerator or freezer.

Brown bread flour

Brown bread flour is made from white bread flour to which approximately 12 per cent fine wheaten bran (a valuable source of fibre) has been added. Brown bread meal is used by commercial bakeries to bake brown bread and domestically primarily for making bread and scones.

Store brown bread flour for

Front row, from left: Soft flour, self-raising flour, white bread flour and semolina.
Back row, from left: Granary flour, brown bread flour and bran.

up to 2 months under ideal conditions, and for up to 1 year in a refrigerator or freezer.

Granary and wholemeal flours

Granary flour, also known as malted wheat, is made from bread flour to which coarse wheaten bran, malt flakes and cracked wheat have been added. Used in scones, breads and rusks, it is one of the most popular of wholemeal flours. These have a high fibre content, which is an essential part of a healthy diet.

Due to the presence of wheat germ, all types of wholemeal flour have an oil content and therefore cannot be stored as long as the white flours. In hot, humid conditions it is always advisable to store such flours in a refrigerator.

When using wholemeal flour on its own in baking, bear in mind that the baked product will be slightly heavier than usual. If you require a lighter texture, replace half the quantity of wholemeal flour with soft or white bread flour.

Store granary and similar flours for up to 2 months under ideal conditions, and for up to 1 year in a refrigerator or freezer.

Semolina

This is a pure wheaten product in granular form that is used commercially for making spaghetti and noodles, and is also ideal for milk puddings and gnocchi. Store for 3–4 months under ideal conditions, and for up to 1 year in a refrigerator or freezer.

Bran

The outer layer of the wheat kernel is removed to produce bran, which is an unrefined by-product of flour. It is rich in cellulose, a type of fibre, and in vitamins and minerals. It can be added to breads, scones and muesli and sprinkled over porridge and cereals. Store for 2 months under ideal conditions, and up to 1 year in a refrigerator or freezer.

Other grains

Different types of flour are also made from other cereals including barley, rye, buckwheat and maize. The roughly milled grain of maize is better known as cornmeal, not to be confused with cornflour, the thickening agent. These flours are usually combined with wheat flour for baking purposes.

STORING FLOUR

● Because flour readily absorbs foreign flavours and odours, it is essential to store it in a clean, airtight container in a cool, dry place, away from any products with a strong flavour or odour. Buy enough flour for the short term only, especially if you live in a hot climate, where weevils and worm infestation are common. Do not add fresh flour to old flour.

● Place a bay leaf in the flour to prevent weevils.

● Every packet of flour is stamped with a 'sell by' date, which should be used as a guide to the age of the flour. The flour may be used for 6–8 months after the date has expired but it is unlikely that a packet would last so long in an average household.

● Store flour in an airtight container in a refrigerator or freezer for up to 1 year. Return to room temperature an hour before using.

● The amount of liquid given in a recipe may have to be adjusted depending on the age of the flour – the fresher the flour, the less liquid you will need; the older the flour, the more liquid you will need.

USEFUL HINTS

How to use the recipes

First read the recipe carefully. Ingredients in recipes always appear in the order in which they are used. For best results in baking, use ingredients at room temperature, unless stated otherwise. Collect and measure all the ingredients, prepare the specified baking tins and set the oven to the correct temperature before beginning.

Correct measuring

Ingredients should be measured or weighed very accurately. To ensure success, use reliable scales and measuring jugs.

Always follow either the metric or imperial measurements given in the recipes as the two systems are *not* interchangeable.

INGREDIENTS

Flour

To measure flour correctly, spoon the unsifted flour gently into the scales (or measuring cup), without pressing down. Shake the cup slightly and level off with a knife or spatula, then sift the flour once before starting to mix, as this will ensure light results.

Plain flour, soft flour, self-raising flour, white bread flour and semolina should be sifted. Brown bread flour and wholemeal flour are also sifted, and the bran left behind in the sieve is tipped back into the flour. Bran cannot be sifted and is therefore just added and stirred into the other ingredients.

Baking powder

In ideal conditions, a tin of commercial baking powder can be stored for 1 year. To extend its shelf life, store baking powder in the refrigerator or freezer.

Eggs

All the recipes in this book were tested using large eggs. Eggs determine the colour, flavour, lightness and binding of the cake mixture, as well as its nutritional value. To ensure freshness, buy small quantities of eggs at a time. Work with eggs that are at room temperature; this will enable you to beat them to a greater volume. When creaming, always add the eggs one at a time and beat well after each addition.

Fat

Either margarine or butter can be used in baking, but where butter is specifically referred to in recipes such as those for pastries, it cannot be replaced by margarine. Butter gives the best flavour, especially to a sponge cake. When baking with margarine, use block margarine and not the tub variety, as the latter contains more water and can easily be over-creamed. In some sponge cakes oil is used.

Chilled margarine or butter is required for pastries and rubbing in. When rubbing into flour, use your fingertips as these are the coolest part of your hands.

For accurate and easy use, measuring is done in grams (ounces). Take margarine or butter out of the refrigerator at least an hour prior to baking. It will then be fairly soft and facilitate easy creaming.

Sugar

White granulated sugar has been used, unless caster sugar or brown sugar is specified. Caster sugar is finer and therefore creams more easily. If no caster sugar is available, grind granulated sugar in a blender or food processor for a few seconds to give a finer texture. When creaming margarine and sugar together, add the sugar a little at a time and cream using either a wooden spoon or an electric mixer. Adding the sugar slowly and gradually will make it possible for the sugar to dissolve more easily. Once all the sugar has been added, beat the mixture until it is light and fluffy. Most of the sugar will dissolve in the creaming process. This will ensure a light texture in a cake or biscuit.

Liquid

Liquid is essential in baking. Apart from combining the ingredients, the liquid forms steam and aids the rising of cakes. Use water, milk, fruit juices and wines at room temperature, unless otherwise stated in the recipe. Measure accurately by placing the measuring jug on a flat surface and checking the level. This will ensure the right consistency in a mixture. Do not add all the liquid at once, but pour slowly into the dry ingredients.

Substitutes

If you do not have any sour milk, add lemon juice to fresh milk in the proportions of 20 ml (4 tsp) to every 250 ml (8 fl oz). Cream may be soured in the same way.

Golden syrup or honey may be substituted for sugar in fruit cakes and similar recipes.

Instant dry yeast is easier to obtain than fresh compressed yeast but this may be used if preferred. When 10 g (⅓ oz) of instant dry yeast is specified, you will find that 25 g (about ¾ oz) of fresh yeast will be needed.

COMPARATIVE OVEN TEMPERATURES

	Celsius (C)	Fahrenheit (F)	Gas mark
Very low:	100 °C	200 °F	–
	110 °C	225 °F	¼
	120 °C	250 °F	½
Low:	140 °C	275 °F	1
	150 °C	300 °F	2
Moderate:	160 °C	325 °F	3
	180 °C	350 °F	4
Moderately high:	190 °C	375 °F	5
	200 °C	400 °F	6
High:	220 °C	425 °F	7
	230 °C	450 °F	8
Very high:	240 °C	475 °F	9

PREHEATING THE OVEN

Before preheating your oven, adjust the shelves to the required level. The temperatures and baking times given in these recipes are only a guideline. Get to know your oven and adjust the temperatures and times accordingly. Turn the oven on at least 10 minutes before baking and set it about 5–10 degrees higher than the temperature required, as when you open the oven door, hot air will escape and the temperature will drop. After placing the cake in the oven, turn the setting to the correct temperature.

If using a fan-assisted oven, you are advised to follow the manufacturer's instructions.

Level of shelves in oven for baking

● The oven is slightly warmer at the top than it is lower down. Pastry is baked on the top and second shelves. If the grill is in the oven, the same shelves are used for toasting and grilling food.

● Bake small cakes or biscuits one shelf above the middle shelf.

● The heat is very even in the middle of the oven and general baking of cakes, breads and biscuits, for example, is done here.

● Large cakes and rich fruit cakes should be baked one shelf below the middle shelf.

● The bottom of the oven is slightly cooler and should be used for slow cooking, for example meringues, as well as for drying rusks.

USING A MICROWAVE

Many different types of microwave ovens are now available, ranging from the most basic worktop ones to quite sophisticated appliances which combine microwave energy with conventional heat.

Manufacturers are constantly adding new features to their models. If you are thinking of buying a microwave oven, it is advisable to consider the extent to which you would make use of such features as these will inevitably increase the cost of the appliance.

Whatever model of microwave you have, it is strongly recommended that you should follow the advice given in the manufacturer's handbook. To achieve the best results, get to know your microwave, as wattage differs from oven to oven, which will affect baking and cooking times.

Higher wattage microwave ovens (600 – 850 watts) are faster than the lower wattage ovens (400 – 500 watts). Ovens with a 650 wattage are more common, so most recipes are developed for these ovens. If your microwave oven is 600 watts, add 15 seconds to cooking time. For a 700 watt oven, subtract 5–10 seconds per minute.

Wattage and power

High	100% power
Medium-High	70% power
Medium	50% power
Medium-Low	30% power
Low	10% power

Testing equipment for microwaving

To establish whether cookware is suitable for microwave use, pour 250 ml (8 fl oz) cold water into a glass bowl or jug. Place this in the microwave, together with the dish to be tested. Microwave on High/100% power for 1 minute. The water in the bowl or jug should be warm, and the dish cool. If the dish is warm, it is not suitable for use in the microwave.

Important guidelines for microwaving

● Owing to the fact that ovens, cake mixtures and containers will differ, an exact time for baking cannot be given. A useful guideline to calculating the time needed for baking is to divide the time given for a conventional oven by four and then subtract a third.

● Lightly grease or spray the container. Place a piece of paper towel cut to size on the base. Do not flour the container.

● Cakes will cook better on a Medium-High/70% power or on a Medium/50% power.

• Take care not to overbake cakes. Remove from oven when just baked and test with a skewer.

• Cup cakes are best baked on Medium/50% power. Do not fill more than half full.

• Muffins can be baked in paper cup cases on Medium-High/70% power for 3–4 minutes (six muffins). Place the paper case in a microwave muffin container or tea cup.

• Bake scones on a preheated browning dish on High/100% for 30 seconds. Turn over and repeat.

• Fill pans only two-thirds full.

CAKE TIN SIZES

Cake tins are made in a wide range of sizes and shapes that may be useful to collect gradually. It is often possible to hire novelty shapes, such as numerals for birthday cakes, from kitchen equipment or cake decorating shops. Cheap tins tend to buckle quickly, so it is worth buying heavier, better quality ones. Non-stick tins vary enormously in quality and the surface is easily scratched if a metal spatula is inadvertently used to spread the mixture. If you are baking in a microwave oven, you must use dishes made of suitable materials as specified in the manufacturer's handbook. For good results, it is advisable to use the type of tin specified in the recipes in this book:

1 **Round cake tin 20 cm (8 inch)**

2 **Loaf tin 23 cm (9 inch)**

3 **Loose-bottomed tart tin 23 cm (9 inch)**

4 **Flan tin 23 cm (9 inch)**

5 **Swiss roll tin 23 x 32 cm (9 x 13 inch)**

6 **Loose-bottomed cake tin 20 cm (8 inch)**

7 **Ring tin 23 cm (9 inch)**

8 **Fluted flan tin 23 cm (9 inch)**

9 **Rectangular tin 20 x 25 cm (8 x 10 inch)**

10 **Square deep cake tin 20 cm (8 inch)**

Handy tips

• Scald milk for use in custards and sauces by heating 625 ml (1 pint) milk on High/100% power for 2–3 minutes.

• Caramelize sugar by placing sugar and water in a heat-resistant bowl. Microwave on High/100% power for 5–7 minutes, until golden.

• Heat golden syrup/honey in a heat-resistant bowl on High/100% power for 1–2 minutes for every 300 g (9½ oz).

• Soften brown sugar by placing in microwave with a wedge of apple. Heat, covered, on High/100% power for 30–40 seconds.

• Liquefy crystallized honey by heating on High/100% power for 30 seconds. Stir until smooth, then microwave for a few more seconds.

• Toast desiccated coconut by microwaving 500 ml on High/100% power for 5–6 minutes. Stir frequently.

• To melt chocolate: Break into pieces and place in a heat-resistant bowl. Microwave on High/100 % power for about 1 minute per 90 g (3 oz). Stir until smooth. Microwave for a few more seconds if still lumpy, taking care not to overheat, or the chocolate will burn.

• Soften 125 g (4 oz) butter on Medium-Low/30% power for 40 seconds.

• To enable yeast dough to rise quickly (to prove): Place the dough in a bowl and cover with cling film. Pour 1 litre (1¾ pints) of warm water into a large bowl. Place the bowl containing the water alongside. Microwave on Low/10% power for 10 minutes. Allow to rest for 15 minutes. Repeat until dough has doubled in size.

● To reheat cooked pastry: Heat small pies on High/100% power for 10–30 seconds and larger pies for 2–3 minutes.

● To defrost a loaf of bread: Wrap in damp paper towel and defrost on Medium-Low/30% power for 4 minutes, depending on the size of the loaf.

● To defrost a slice of bread: Wrap in damp paper towel and heat on High/100% power for 10–15 seconds.

● To blanch almonds: Cover 125 g (4 oz) nuts with 150 ml (½ pint) water and microwave on High/100% for about 2 minutes. Drain, and the skins will slip off.

● Warm oranges or lemons on High/100% for 30–60 seconds before squeezing to produce more juice.

● Cover dried fruit with water and microwave on High/100% for about 5 minutes until plump and soft. Then stir and leave to stand for 5 minutes. Drain well before using.

Notes

In the United Kingdom and New Zealand a tablespoon is the equivalent of 15 ml as specified in the recipes.

In Australia a tablespoon is the equivalent of 20 ml.

A few terms and ingredients used in this book may not be familiar to readers in Australia and New Zealand. The following list may therefore be helpful.

aubergine: eggplant
bacon (streaky): lower end of smoked back
chocolate (plain): dark chocolate
cling film: plastic wrap
courgette: baby marrow
cream, single: thin cream
cream, double: thick cream
curd cheese: smooth cottage cheese
demerara sugar: substitute raw sugar
granulated sugar: white sugar
pepper, green: sweet (bell) pepper
haddock (fresh): substitute gemfish or hake
haddock (smoked): substitute smoked cod
mixed dried fruit: fruit cake mix
spring onion: green shallot

ALTITUDE BAKING

For the purposes of this book, all the recipes were tested at different altitudes as well as at sea level. The following chart is therefore not necessary for recipes in this book, but can be used to make adjustments in other recipes you may have. High altitude recipes can be used in reverse.

ALTITUDE	900 m (3000 ft)	1500 m (5000 ft)	2100 m (7000 ft)	3000 m (10000 ft)
Temperature	Increase by 5 °C/25 °F	Increase by 10 °C/50 °F	Increase by 10 °C/50 °F	Increase by 10 °C/50 °F
Baking powder per 5 ml (1 tsp)	Reduce by small pinch	Reduce by pinch	Reduce by pinch	Reduce by pinch
Sugar per 250 g (8 oz)	Reduce by 0–15 ml (0–1 tbsp)	Reduce by 15–30 ml (1–2 tbsp)	Reduce by 30–45 ml (2–3 tbsp)	Reduce by 30–45 ml (2–3 tbsp)
Liquid per 250 ml (8 fl oz)	Increase by 0–30 ml (0–2 tbsp)	Increase by 30–45 ml (2–3 tbsp)	Increase by 45–60 ml (3–4 tbsp)	Increase by 45–60 ml (3–4 tbsp)
Flour per 150 g (5 oz)			Increase by 15 ml (1 tbsp)	Increase by 15 ml (1 tbsp)

USING 250 ML MEASURING CUP

As anyone who uses 250 ml measuring cups rather than scales will be aware, the density factor of different ingredients varies considerably. The approximate weight in grams of the principal ingredients used in the recipes is given in the list below.

All Bran Flakes/Cornflakes	50	Flour	150
Breadcrumbs		Golden syrup	375
dried	125	Ham, chopped	125
fresh	60	Jam	340
Carrots, grated	125	Nuts	150
Cheese:		Oats	90
Cheddar, grated	125	Pineapple, crushed	165
cottage and cream	250	Pumpkin, cooked, mashed	210
Mozzarella, grated	125	Seeds:	
Cherries, glacé	180	sunflower/poppy/sesame	150
Chocolate chips	210	Semolina	165
Coconut, desiccated	90	Spinach, cooked	180
Dried fruit:		Sugar:	
apricots	150	brown	180
currants	150	caster	250
dates	150	granulated	250
mixed	180	icing	180
mixed peel	180		
prunes, stoned	180		
raisins	180		
sultanas	180		

MANY OF THESE QUICK-AND-EASY SAVOURIES AND SNACKS CAN ALSO BE SERVED AS LIGHT MEALS, AND MOST CAN BE CONVENIENTLY PREPARED IN ADVANCE AND HEATED WHEN REQUIRED. VERSATILE PIZZAS, SAVOURY TARTS AND QUICHES CAN BE MADE IN DIFFERENT SIZES WITH A VARIETY OF TOPPINGS AND, SERVED INDIVIDUALLY, ARE IDEAL AS STARTERS. AS AN ORDINARY BREAD OR SCONE DOUGH IS USED, PIZZAS COULDN'T BE EASIER TO MAKE – AND THE RESULTS ARE EXCELLENT!

MUSHROOM AND BACON QUICHE

PASTRY
135 g (4½ oz) plain flour
125 g (4 oz) grated Cheddar cheese
125 g (4 oz) butter

FILLING
250 g (8 oz) streaky bacon, chopped
15 g (½ oz) butter
200 g (6½ oz) mushrooms, sliced
3 eggs
250 ml (8 fl oz) milk or single cream
125 ml (4 fl oz) soured cream
15 ml (1 tbsp) lemon juice
45 ml (3 tbsp) grated Parmesan cheese
2.5 ml (½ tsp) mustard powder
2.5 ml (½ tsp) salt
freshly ground black pepper to taste
5 ml (1 tsp) chopped fresh herbs OR
2.5 ml (½ tsp) mixed dried herbs

❶ For pastry: Mix all ingredients to a soft pastry in a food processor.

❷ Press into base and sides of 23 cm (9 inch) quiche dish.

❸ For filling: Fry bacon until crisp. Remove and keep aside. Add butter to rendered fat. Add mushrooms and sauté; spoon bacon and mushrooms on to base. Beat eggs, milk, soured cream and lemon juice. Add Parmesan cheese and seasoning; pour on to base.

❹ Bake in a preheated oven at 160 °C (325 °F/gas 3) for 45 minutes.

Serves 4–6

TIP

The difference between quiches and savoury tarts is that quiches have a savoury egg custard mixture as a base, whereas savoury tarts can have a starch, such as cornflour or flour, with or without an egg, to bind the mixture.

SALMON AND LEEK QUICHE

PASTRY
135 g (4½ oz) plain flour
125 g (4 oz) Cheddar cheese, grated
125 g (4 oz) butter

FILLING
15 g (½ oz) butter
4 leeks, sliced
2 cloves garlic, crushed
210 g (7 oz) can pink salmon, flaked
3 eggs
250 ml (8 fl oz) milk or single cream
125 ml (4 fl oz) soured cream
15 ml (1 tbsp) lemon juice
2.5 ml (½ tsp) salt
freshly ground black pepper to taste
5 ml (1 tsp) chopped fresh herbs OR
2.5 ml (½ tsp) mixed dried herbs

❶ For pastry: Mix all ingredients to a soft pastry in a food processor.

❷ Press into base and sides of 23 cm (9 inch) quiche dish.

❸ For filling: Heat butter and sauté leeks and garlic. Mix in salmon and spoon onto base. Beat eggs, milk, soured cream and lemon juice. Add seasoning and pour onto base.

❹ Bake in a preheated oven at 160 °C (325 °F/gas 3) for 45 minutes.

Serves 4–6

TIP

Clean leeks by cutting through the leek down its length, almost through the root, and again a second time, making a cross. Open out and wash thoroughly under cold running waterwater. Cut into rings.

ASPARAGUS ONION TART

PASTRY
135 g (4½ oz) plain flour
5 ml (1 tsp) salt
125 g (4 oz) margarine
225 g (7½ oz) can creamed sweetcorn

FILLING
5 medium onions, chopped
60 g (2 oz) margarine
180 g (6 oz) Cheddar cheese, grated
2.5 ml (½ tsp) salt
2 eggs, beaten
250 ml (8 fl oz) soured cream
400 g (13 oz) can asparagus (salad cuts), drained

❶ For pastry: Sift flour and salt. Rub in margarine until mixture resembles fine breadcrumbs. Add sweetcorn and mix well. Spread into base and sides of a greased 23 cm (9 inch) ovenproof pie dish.

❷ For filling: Sauté onion in margarine until transparent.

❸ Add remaining ingredients, mix well, and spoon onto prepared base.

❹ Bake in a preheated oven at 180 °C (350 °F/gas 4) for 45–60 minutes, or until set and golden brown.

Serves 4–6

TIP

To prevent irritation of the eyes, peel onions under cold running water. Alternatively, place onions in cold water 30 minutes before peeling.

Clockwise from top right: Salmon and Leek Quiche, Asparagus Onion Tart and Mushroom and Bacon Quiche.

HAM AND PINEAPPLE PIZZA

BASE
280 g (9 oz) self-raising flour
30 g (1 oz) margarine
about 200 ml (6½ fl oz) milk

TOPPING
400 g (13 oz) can tomato-onion mix
15 ml (1 tbsp) chopped fresh oregano
OR
5 ml (1 tsp) dried
15 ml (1 tbsp) chopped fresh basil OR
5 ml (1 tsp) dried
pinch salt
2 cloves garlic, crushed, optional
freshly ground black pepper to taste
1 green pepper, seeded and thinly sliced
440 g (14 oz) can pineapple pieces, drained
250 g (8 oz) smoked ham, chopped
250 g (8 oz) mozzarella cheese, grated OR Cheddar cheese

❶ For base: Sift flour and rub in margarine.

❷ Add milk and mix to form a soft dough.

❸ Divide dough in half and roll out to fit two greased 25 cm (10 inch) pizza plates or place on a large greased baking tray.

❹ For topping: Heat tomato-onion mix, seasoning and garlic in a saucepan. Simmer for a few minutes and spread onto base.

❺ Top with remaining ingredients and sprinkle with grated mozzarella or Cheddar cheese.

❻ Bake in a preheated oven at 200 °C (400 °F/gas 6) for 20–25 minutes or until golden brown.

Makes 2 large pizzas

VARIATION

Replace ham with sliced pepperoni sausage.

TIP

If serving pizzas as snacks, cut into squares once cooked, or make small individual ones.

TOMATO AND MUSHROOM PIZZA

BASE
280 g (9 oz) plain flour
2.5 ml (½ tsp) salt
2.5 ml (½ tsp) sugar
7.5 ml (1½ tsp) instant dry yeast
30 ml (2 tbsp) cooking oil
about 125 ml (4 fl oz) lukewarm water

TOPPING
400 g (13 oz) can tomato-onion mix
2 cloves garlic, crushed
1 green pepper, seeded and sliced
250 g (8 oz) mushrooms, sliced
125 g (4 oz) salami slices
5 ml (1 tsp) dried Italian seasoning OR dried oregano
5 ml (1 tsp) salt
freshly ground black pepper to taste
125 g (4 oz) mozzarella cheese, grated OR Cheddar cheese

❶ For base: Sift flour and salt. Add sugar and dry yeast and mix.

❷ Add oil and enough lukewarm water to mix to a soft dough. Knead for 5–10 minutes until dough is smooth and elastic.

❸ Cover with oiled cling film and leave in a warm place for 45 minutes to rise, until double in volume.

❹ Knock down and divide into two. Flatten and place each piece on a greased 25 cm (10 inch) pizza plate.

❺ For topping: Heat tomato-onion mix, add garlic and green pepper and simmer for a few minutes. Spread on to base. Top with remaining ingredients and sprinkle with grated cheese. Leave to rest for 20 minutes.

❻ Bake in a preheated oven at 200 °C (400 °F/gas 6) for 20 minutes.

Makes 2 large pizzas

VARIATIONS

Substitute chopped ham, bacon or tuna for salami.

Add or substitute other ingredients of your choice, such as pineapple, shrimps, asparagus and olives.

TIP

Pizzas on a yeast dough base, baked or unbaked, can be frozen successfully for up to one month, provided topping ingredients are suitable for freezing. Bake frozen, cooked pizza in a preheated oven at 200 °C (400 °F/gas 6) for 15 minutes and frozen uncooked pizza for 30 minutes.

MUSHROOMS IN BATTER

1 egg
250 ml (8 fl oz) milk
150 g (5 oz) self-raising flour
10 ml (2 tsp) mixed spice
5 ml (1 tsp) salt
freshly ground black pepper to taste
1 clove garlic, crushed
250 g (8 oz) button mushrooms

❶ Whisk egg and milk together. Sift dry ingredients and add milk mixture and crushed garlic to dry ingredients.

❷ Beat until smooth and leave batter standing for 30 minutes. (Batter can be kept in refrigerator for 1–2 weeks.)

❸ Dip mushrooms in batter and deep-fry in hot oil until golden brown.

❹ Drain on paper towels.

Serves 4–6

VARIATION

Substitute onion rings, cauliflower florets or broccoli florets for mushrooms.

TIP

Keep garlic fresh by peeling and placing in a bottle. Cover with olive or sunflower oil. Replace lid and refrigerate until needed. The oil can also be used for flavouring salads and meat.

Clockwise from top right: Ham and Pineapple Pizza, Tomato and Mushroom Pizza and miniature Tomato and Mushroom Pizzas.

CHEESE TART

PASTRY
210 g (7 oz) plain flour
2.5 ml (½ tsp) salt
1 egg, beaten
90 g (3 oz) butter
about 45 ml (3 tbsp) water

FILLING
4 eggs, separated
250 ml (8 fl oz) single cream
125 g (4 oz) smoked ham, chopped
135 g (4½ oz) Cheddar cheese, grated
2.5 ml (½ tsp) paprika
2.5 ml (½ tsp) mustard powder
15 ml (1 tbsp) chopped fresh herbs
OR 5 ml (1 tbsp) mixed dried herbs
2.5 ml (½ tsp) salt
freshly ground black pepper to taste

❶ For pastry: Sift flour and salt. Add beaten egg and mix well.

❷ Grate cold butter over mixture and knead lightly. Add water, if necessary, and mix to a soft dough.

❸ Cover pastry with oiled cling film and leave to rest in the refrigerator for 30 minutes. Roll out thinly, line base and sides of a 23 cm (9 inch) pie dish with pastry and prick base. Cover and leave in the refrigerator while preparing the filling.

❹ For filling: Mix egg yolks, cream, ham, cheese and seasoning.

❺ Beat egg whites until soft peak stage and fold into egg yolk mixture.

❻ Pour onto base and bake in a preheated oven at 160 °C (325 °F/gas 3) for 45 minutes. Cover with foil during baking if tart starts to brown.

Serves 4–6

TIP

Cheese can be grated and stored in an airtight container in the freezer for up to 6 months.

15

CHEESE STRAWS

½ quantity Puff Pastry (page 32)
125 g (4 oz) Cheddar cheese, grated
2.5 ml (½ tsp) salt
2.5 ml (½ tsp) cayenne pepper

❶ Roll out pastry in a rectangular shape, to a thickness of 3 mm (⅛ inch).

❷ Sprinkle grated cheese, salt and pepper over two-thirds of pastry. Fold up like a business letter so that cheese is sandwiched between layers of pastry. Refrigerate for 30 minutes.

❸ Roll out to a thickness of 3 mm (⅛ inch). Cut into strips of 1.5 cm x 7.5 cm (½ x 3 inches). Twist each one and place on a greased baking tray.

❹ Bake in a preheated oven at 200 °C (400 °F/gas 6) for 10 minutes.

Makes about 70

CHEESE AIGRETTES

125 g (4 oz) Cheddar cheese, grated
1 quantity Choux Pastry (page 33)
cooking oil for frying
cayenne pepper

❶ Add grated cheese to choux pastry.

❷ Fry teaspoonfuls in deep, hot oil for 3–5 minutes, or until golden brown.

❸ Drain on paper towels and sprinkle with cayenne pepper.

Makes 20

VARIATIONS

POTATO PUFFS

Add 1 medium mashed potato and 5 ml (1 tsp) mixed dried herbs to ingredients.

MINCE AND SWEETCORN AIGRETTES

Omit cheese and add 150 g (5 oz) cooked topside mince and a 225 g (7½ oz) can creamed sweetcorn to pastry.

FRIED PASTIES

500 g (1 lb) topside mince
15 ml (1 tbsp) cooking oil
1 onion, finely chopped
1 clove garlic, crushed
1 carrot, finely grated
1 potato, finely grated
5 ml (1 tsp) ground allspice
7.5 ml (1½ tsp) salt
freshly ground black pepper to taste
200 ml (6½ fl oz) meat stock
2 quantities Shortcrust Pastry (page 30) OR
2 quantities Soda-water Pastry (page 32)
whole cloves
cooking oil for frying

❶ Fry the meat in oil until its colour changes. Add the onion and garlic and sauté.

❷ Add carrot, potato, allspice, seasoning and meat stock and simmer for 15 minutes. Leave to cool.

❸ Roll out pastry to a thickness of 3 mm (⅛ inch). Cut into 7.5 x 7.5 cm (3 x 3 inch) squares. Place a little meat mixture in centre. Fold the four corners towards the centre and secure with a clove.

❹ Deep-fry in oil until golden brown. Drain on paper towels and serve hot.

Makes 48

TIP

If the chopping board you are using smells of onions or garlic, mark one side of the board with a pen and chop them on that side only.

COCKTAIL SAUSAGE ROLLS

30 ml (2 tbsp) cooking oil
600 g (1¼ lb) topside mince
1 onion, finely chopped
3 slices white bread, soaked in water
5 ml (1 tsp) salt
freshly ground black pepper to taste
pinch ground cloves
2.5 ml (½ tsp) ground coriander
1 beef stock cube
20 ml (4 tsp) vinegar
1 quantity Soda-water Pastry (page 32) OR
1 quantity Hot-water Pastry (page 32)
beaten egg or milk to glaze

❶ Heat oil and fry mince until colour changes. Add onion and sauté slightly.

❷ Add soaked bread, seasoning, spices, stock cube and vinegar. Simmer for about 5 minutes. Leave to cool completely.

❸ Roll out pastry into a rectangular shape about 10 cm (4 inches) wide. Place meat in a line down the middle. Fold one side of pastry over meat. Brush edge with water and cover with other side of pastry. Brush with beaten egg or milk.

❹ Cut into sections of about 4 cm (1½ inches) and bake in a preheated oven at 200 °C (400 °F/gas 6) for 20 minutes.

Makes 48

TIP

Use 45 ml (3 tbsp) home-made stock instead of the stock cube, as stock cubes have a high salt content.

Clockwise from top: Cheese Straws, Cocktail Sausage Rolls, Fried Pasties, Cheese Aigrettes and Mince and Sweetcorn Aigrettes.

VOL-AU-VENT CASES

1 quantity Puff Pastry (page 32)
beaten egg or milk to glaze

❶ Roll out pastry to a thickness of 3 mm (⅛ inch). Use a 10 cm (4 inch) cutter to cut out 12–16 circles. Use a smaller cutter to cut out the centre of half of these circles to make lids.

❷ Brush edges of full circles with water. Place ones with centre cut out on top. Press down lightly.

❸ Brush with beaten egg or milk. Place on a greased baking tray and bake in a preheated oven at 200 °C (400 °F/gas 6) for 20 minutes, until golden brown. Bake lids at the same time.

❹ Hollow out centre slightly and fill, placing lids on top.

Makes 6–8

VARIATION

Bouchées, a smaller version of vol-au-vent cases, are made in the same way, without the pastry lid.

TIP

Before placing the vol-au-vent cases in the oven, prick each top layer four times with a skewer to ensure that the sides of the cases rise evenly.

Mushroom and chicken filling

30 g (1 oz) margarine
30 ml (2 tbsp) plain flour
250 ml (8 fl oz) milk
110 g (3½ oz) mushrooms, chopped
125 g (4 oz) cooked chicken, finely chopped
2.5 ml (½ tsp) salt
freshly ground black pepper to taste

❶ Melt margarine in a saucepan. Add flour and stir over low heat for 1 minute. Remove from heat and add milk, stirring until smooth.

❷ Return to medium heat and stir constantly until boiling. Lower heat and cook for 5 minutes, stirring frequently until thickened.

❸ Add the mushrooms, chicken and seasoning. Fill vol-au-vent cases or bouchées and serve while still hot.

Tuna and cucumber filling

200 g (6½ oz) can solid tuna, in vegetable oil, drained and flaked
½ cucumber, diced
1 spring onion, chopped
about 75 ml (5 tbsp) mayonnaise
15 ml (1 tbsp) chopped fresh parsley OR 5 ml (1 tsp) dried
pinch salt
freshly ground black pepper to taste

Mix all ingredients together and fill vol-au-vent cases.

BANANA BACON ROLLS

2 bananas
30 ml (2 tbsp) lemon juice
½ quantity flaky pastry (page 32)
125 g (4 oz) rindless streaky bacon
beaten egg or milk to glaze

❶ Cut each banana in half horizontally and each half into five pieces. Dip pieces in lemon juice.

❷ Roll out pastry to a thickness of 3 mm (⅛ inch). Cut into strips long enough to wrap around banana pieces.

❸ Wrap each piece of banana in a rasher of bacon and cover with pastry strip. Damp end with water to seal.

❹ Place on a greased baking tray and brush with beaten egg or milk.

❺ Bake in a preheated oven at 220 °C (425 °F/gas 7) for 20 minutes. Serve hot.

Makes 20

QUICK SAVOURY TART

250 g (8 oz) rindless streaky bacon, chopped
1 onion, chopped
250 g (8 oz) button mushrooms, sliced
15 g (½ oz) butter
30 ml (2 tbsp) chopped fresh herbs OR 10 ml (2 tsp) mixed dried herbs
freshly ground black pepper to taste
250 g (8 oz) Cheddar cheese, grated
2 eggs
250 ml (8 fl oz) milk
45 ml (3 tbsp) self-raising flour

❶ Fry bacon in a saucepan. Add onion, mushrooms and butter and sauté lightly.

❷ Add herbs and pepper to above ingredients and layer on bottom of a greased 18 x 28 cm (7 x 11 inch) ovenproof dish. Sprinkle with grated cheese.

❸ Beat eggs, milk and flour together and pour over ingredients in dish.

❹ Bake in a preheated oven at 180 °C (350 °F/gas 4) for 30 minutes, or until set and golden brown.

Serves 4–6

TIP

Fry streaky bacon by placing it in a cold frying pan, without fat. Cook over low heat, turning frequently, until done to your liking. For crisp bacon, pour off the fat as it collects.

From top: Quick Savoury Tart, Banana Bacon Rolls, Vol-au-vent Cases and Bouchees.

2

LIGHT MEALS

THE RECIPES IN THIS SECTION REQUIRE VERY LITTLE PREPARATION TIME AND PRODUCE TASTY, ECONOMICAL DISHES THAT ARE IDEAL FOR LIGHT SUPPERS OR LUNCHES — AND MANY WILL APPEAL TO THE WEIGHT-CONSCIOUS. INCLUDED ARE A VARIETY OF DELICIOUS HOME-MADE PIES — WHICH ARE ALWAYS NICER THAN COMMERCIALLY MADE — AS WELL AS FISH PIES, A SOUFFLE AND MINCE DISHES.

HADDOCK PIE

30 g (1 oz) margarine
30 ml (2 tbsp) plain flour
250 ml (8 fl oz) milk
250 g (8 oz) frozen haddock fillets,
cooked and flaked
125 g (4 oz) Cheddar cheese, grated
15 ml (1 tbsp) chopped gherkins
1 medium onion, finely chopped
15 ml (1 tbsp) chopped fresh parsley
OR 5 ml (1 tsp) dried
15 ml (1 tbsp) chopped fresh herbs
OR 5 ml (1 tsp) dried mixed herbs
5 ml (1 tsp) mustard powder
2.5 ml (½ tsp) salt
freshly ground black pepper to taste
3 eggs, beaten
1 quantity Cream Cheese Pastry
(page 34)

❶ Melt margarine in a saucepan. Add flour and stir over low heat for 1 minute. Remove from heat and add milk, stirring until smooth.

❷ Return to medium heat and stir constantly until boiling. Lower heat and cook for 5 minutes, stirring frequently. Remove from heat.

❸ Add remaining ingredients, except pastry, to white sauce.

❹ Roll out pastry to a thickness of 3 mm (⅛ inch) and line a greased, round 23 cm (9 inch) pie dish.

❺ Spoon filling onto base and bake in a preheated oven at 180 °C (350 °F/gas 4) for 30 minutes.

Serves 4–6

TIP

To cook haddock in the microwave: Place fish in a small dish and add a little water. Cover and microwave for 3–4 minutes on High 100% power.

STEAK AND KIDNEY PIE

180 g (6 oz) calf or lamb's kidneys
500 g (1 lb) topside
15 g (½ oz) butter
15 ml (1 tbsp) cooking oil
1 onion, chopped
375 ml (12 fl oz) meat stock
15 ml (1 tbsp) vinegar
5 ml (1 tsp) salt
freshly ground black pepper to taste
15 ml (1 tbsp) chopped fresh herbs
OR 5 ml (1 tsp) mixed dried herbs
25 ml (5 tsp) plain flour
½ quantity Soda-water Pastry
(page 32) OR
½ quantity Shortcrust Pastry
(page 30)
beaten egg or milk to glaze

❶ Prepare kidneys: Make a small cut in the outer membrane and peel away from kidney. Slice kidney in half lengthways and cut out core with scissors or a sharp knife.

❷ Cut meat and kidneys into cubes and brown in heated butter and oil.

❸ Add onion and sauté. Add heated stock, vinegar and seasoning.

❹ Cover with lid and simmer for 30 minutes. Thicken with flour. Place filling in a medium pie dish or six small ones and leave to cool.

❺ Roll out pastry to a thickness of 3 mm (⅛ inch) and cover filling. Brush with beaten egg or milk. Bake in a pre-heated oven at 200 °C (400 °F/gas 6) for 20 minutes.

Serves 4

CORNISH PASTIES

These pasties were originally developed in the 19th century as a convenient lunch for Cornish miners to carry to work in their pockets. Each man's initials were placed on a corner of the pasty so that, if called away, he could return to his own pie.

250 g (8 oz) rump steak
1 medium carrot
1 medium potato
1 medium onion, chopped
15 ml (1 tbsp) chopped fresh parsley
OR 5 ml (1 tsp) dried
15 ml (1 tbsp) chopped fresh herbs
OR 5 ml (1 tsp) mixed dried herbs
5 ml (1 tsp) salt
freshly ground black pepper to taste
30 g (1 oz) butter
1½ quantities Shortcrust Pastry
(page 30) OR
1½ quantities Hot-water Pastry
(page 32)
beaten egg or milk to glaze

❶ Cut meat into cubes of 1.5 x 1.5 cm (½ x ½ inch). Dice carrot and potato. Mix together meat, vegetables and seasoning.

❷ Roll out pastry to a thickness of 3 mm (⅛ inch). Use a saucer to cut out six circles, each about 20 cm (8 inches) in diameter.

❸ Divide meat mixture between pasties, placing it in the centre. Place knob of butter on each.

❹ Dampen edges of pastry with water, bring together over middle of filling, and seal to enclose filling.

❺ Place pasties on a greased baking tray and brush with beaten egg or milk. Bake in a preheated oven at 200 °C (400 °F/gas 6) for 20 minutes. Reduce heat to 150 °C (300 °F/gas 2) and bake for a further 35 minutes.

Makes 6

Clockwise from top right: Haddock Pie, Cornish Pasties and Steak and Kidney Pie.

VEGETABLE MIX WITH DUMPLINGS

30 ml (2 tbsp) cooking oil
3 large potatoes, cut into cubes
2 medium onions, sliced
20 ml (4 tsp) plain flour
5 ml (1 tsp) salt
freshly ground black pepper to taste
250 ml (8 fl oz) chicken stock
2 medium tomatoes, skinned and chopped
3 courgettes, sliced
2 celery sticks, sliced
2 leeks, sliced
180 g (6 oz) button mushrooms, halved

HERB DUMPLINGS
150 g (5 oz) self-raising flour
2.5 ml (½ tsp) salt
30 g (1 oz) margarine
30 ml (2 tbsp) chopped fresh herbs
OR 10 ml (2 tsp) mixed dried herbs
about 125 ml (4 fl oz) milk or water to mix

❶ Heat oil and fry potatoes and onions until golden brown. Add flour, salt, pepper and chicken stock.

❷ Add remaining vegetables and simmer over low heat for 10 minutes.

❸ For dumplings: Sift flour and salt.

❹ Rub in margarine with fingertips until mixture resembles breadcrumbs. Add mixed herbs.

❺ Add enough milk to mix to a soft dough.

❻ Drop spoonfuls of dough onto boiling vegetables.

❼ Cover with lid and boil for another 15 minutes. Do not remove lid until dumplings are cooked.

Serves 4

VARIATIONS FOR DUMPLINGS

Add 5 ml (1 tsp) curry powder to dry ingredients.

Add 2.5 ml (½ tsp) crushed garlic to liquid for mixing.

Add 25 ml (5 tsp) tomato purée or sauce to liquid for mixing.

MINCE ROLL

FILLING
30 ml (2 tbsp) cooking oil
400 g (13 oz) topside mince
1 onion, chopped
2 cloves garlic, crushed
salt and freshly ground black pepper to taste
30 ml (2 tbsp) chopped fresh parsley
OR 10 ml (2 tsp) dried
260 g (8½ oz) chutney

DOUGH
280 g (9 oz) self-raising flour
2.5 ml (½ tsp) salt
5 ml (1 tsp) sugar
30 g (1 oz) margarine
60 g (2 oz) Cheddar cheese, grated
1 egg
125 ml (4 fl oz) milk
beaten egg or milk to glaze

❶ For filling: Heat oil and fry mince until colour changes. Add onion and garlic and sauté a few minutes. Season with salt, pepper and parsley.

❷ Add chutney and leave the filling to cool slightly.

❸ For dough: Sift flour, salt and sugar. Rub in margarine and add cheese.

❹ Beat egg and milk, add to dry ingredients, and mix to a soft dough.

❺ Roll out into a 20 x 30 cm (8 x 12 inch) rectangle. Spoon meat onto dough, roll up like a Swiss roll, and place on a greased baking tray. Make a few incisions in roll. Brush with beaten egg or milk.

❻ Bake in a preheated oven at 180 °C (350 °F/gas 4) for 50 minutes.

Serves 4–6

TIP

Cut roll into 2.5 cm (1 inch) slices, freeze, and bake as required.

CHICKEN PIE

1 chicken or chicken pieces (about 725 g/1½ lb)
250 ml (8 fl oz) chicken stock
bouquet garni
5 ml (1 tsp) salt
freshly ground black pepper to taste
pinch ground cloves
30 g (1 oz) margarine
1 onion, chopped
180 g (6 oz) mushrooms, halved
45 ml (3 tbsp) dry white wine
25 ml (5 tsp) plain flour
150 g (5 oz) frozen peas
½ quantity Shortcrust Pastry (page 30) OR
½ quantity Puff Pastry (page 32)
beaten egg or milk to glaze

❶ In large saucepan, simmer chicken in stock with bouquet garni until cooked and tender.

❷ Remove chicken and bouquet garni from stock. Reserve liquid. Skin, bone and cut chicken meat into small pieces. Add seasoning.

❸ Heat margarine in a heavy-based saucepan and sauté onion and mushrooms lightly.

❹ Heat cooking liquid and wine. Add chicken and mushrooms. Simmer about 15 minutes. Make a paste with flour, thicken sauce, and add peas.

❺ Spoon into a large ovenproof dish or four individual bowls.

❻ Roll out pastry thinly and cover chicken. Trim edges. Brush top with beaten egg or milk and bake in a preheated oven at 200 °C (400 °F/gas 6) for 20 minutes.

Serves 4

TIPS

A bouquet garni is a bunch of herbs – normally a few parsley stalks, a sprig of thyme and a bayleaf – tied together with string or wrapped in muslin and then tied together. Place bundle in dish during cooking, and remove before serving.

Cut a lid for a single pie crust as follows: Invert the pie dish onto the rolled-out pastry and cut around the edge with a sharp knife.

Clockwise from top right: Vegetable Mix with Dumplings, Chicken Pie and Mince Roll.

SAVOURY MINCE DISH

BASE
110 g (3½ oz) mashed potato
110 g (3½ oz) butter or margarine
150 g (5 oz) plain flour
5 ml (1 tsp) baking powder
2.5 ml (½ tsp) salt
1 egg, beaten

FILLING
250 g (8 oz) topside mince
20 ml (4 tsp) cooking oil
1 onion, finely chopped
2 cloves garlic, crushed
150 ml (¼ pint) soured cream
125 ml (4 fl oz) milk
3 eggs
125 g (4 oz) Cheddar cheese, grated
15 ml (1 tbsp) chopped fresh parsley OR 5 ml (1 tsp) dried
5 ml (1 tsp) chopped fresh herbs OR 2.5 ml (½ tsp) mixed dried herbs
2.5 ml (½ tsp) salt
freshly ground black pepper to taste

❶ For base: Mix all ingredients. Press into base and sides of a greased 23 cm (9 inch) round pie dish.

❷ For filling: Fry mince in heated oil until colour changes. Add onion and garlic and sauté lightly.

❸ Beat soured cream, milk and eggs together. Add remaining ingredients and spoon into base.

❹ Bake in a preheated oven at 180 °C (350 °F/gas 4) for 35 minutes.

Serves 4–6

VARIATION

Substitute 250 g (8 oz) bresaola (dried salt lean beef) for the topside mince. Omit the salt from the filling.

TIP

Fresh parsley can be quickly and neatly chopped in a cup or glass using a pair of sharp kitchen scissors.

STEAK PARCELS

4 fillet steaks, 3 cm (1¼ inches) thick
2.5 ml (½ tsp) salt
freshly ground black pepper to taste

FILLING
15 g (½ oz) butter or margarine
1 onion, finely chopped
1 clove garlic, crushed
180 g (6 oz) mushrooms, chopped
2.5 ml (½ tsp) ml salt
freshly ground black pepper to taste

1 quantity Cream Cheese Pastry
(page 34)
beaten egg or milk to glaze

❶ Heat a griddle pan and brown steaks on both sides. Season, place on paper towels, and leave to cool slightly.

❷ For filling: Heat butter and sauté onion, garlic and mushrooms. Add seasoning and leave to cool.

❸ Roll out pastry to a thickness of 3 mm (⅛ inch). Cut into large enough squares for steak and filling. Place steak in middle and top with filling.

❹ Bring four corners together and seal. Brush with beaten egg or milk.

❺ Place on a greased baking tray and bake in a preheated oven at 200 °C (400 °F/gas 6) for 20–25 minutes.

Serves 4

TIP

A lean, tender cut of beef, fillet can be roasted whole or served as steaks.

BEEF STROGANOFF

25 ml (5 tsp) cooking oil
15 g (1 oz) margarine
1 kg (2 lb) topside, cut into strips
60 g (2 oz) plain flour
1 onion, finely chopped
1 clove garlic, crushed
250 g (8 oz) mushrooms, halved
5 ml (1 tsp) salt
freshly ground black pepper to taste
250 ml (8 fl oz) meat stock
250 ml (8 fl oz) soured cream

❶ Heat oil and margarine. Roll beef strips in flour and brown. Add onion and garlic, and sauté.

❷ Stir in mushrooms, salt and pepper and meat stock. Cover and simmer for about 30 minutes, until tender.

❸ Reduce heat, add soured cream, and simmer for a few minutes. Serve immediately.

Serves 4–6

VARIATION

For a low-calorie meal, substitute low-fat plain yoghurt for soured cream.

FISH IN BEER BATTER

150 ml (5 oz) self-raising flour
5 ml (1 tsp) salt
15 ml (1 tbsp) chopped fresh herbs
OR 5 ml (1 tsp) mixed dried herbs
15 ml (1 tbsp) cooking oil
250 ml (8 fl oz) beer
extra flour for coating
725 g (1½ lb) frozen hake fillets
cooking oil for frying

❶ Sift flour and salt. Add dried herbs, oil and beer.

❷ Coat fish with extra flour, dip into batter, and fry in shallow oil. Drain on paper towels.

❸ Serve with Tartare Sauce.

Tartare sauce

250 ml (8 fl oz) mayonnaise
2 eggs, hard-boiled and finely chopped
10 ml (2 tsp) finely chopped gherkins, optional
2 spring onions, finely chopped
15 ml (1 tbsp) chopped fresh parsley OR 5 ml (1 tsp) dried
15 ml (1 tbsp) chopped fresh tarragon OR 5 ml (1 tsp) dried

Mix all ingredients together well, cover and chill in refrigerator until ready to serve.

Serves 4

SAVOURY PUMPKIN PIE

1 quantity Cream Cheese Pastry
(page 34)

FILLING
15 g (½ oz) butter
1 onion, finely chopped
3 rashers rindless streaky bacon, chopped
340 g (11 oz) mashed, cooled pumpkin
60 g (2 oz) Cheddar cheese, grated
3 eggs
90 ml (6 tbsp) fresh milk OR single cream
15 ml (1 tbsp) chopped fresh parsley OR 5 ml (1 tsp) dried
2.5 ml (½ tsp) salt
freshly ground black pepper to taste

❶ Press pastry into base and sides of a 23 cm (9 inch) ovenproof pie dish.

❷ For filling: Heat butter and sauté onion and bacon. Place in a bowl and cool slightly. Add pumpkin and cheese.

❸ Beat eggs and milk and add, with seasoning, to pumpkin mixture. Spoon onto base.

❹ Bake in a preheated oven at 180 °C (350 °F/gas 4) for 45–50 minutes.

Serves 4–6

TIP

Drain pumpkin well before mashing.

Clockwise from top right: Steak Parcels, Fish in Beer Batter and Savoury Pumpkin Pie.

CHEESE SOUFFLE

30 g (1 oz) butter or margarine
30 ml (2 tbsp) plain flour
250 ml (8 fl oz) milk
2.5 ml (½ tsp) salt
freshly ground black pepper to taste
125 g (4 oz) Cheddar cheese, grated
4 eggs, separated

❶ Melt butter or margarine in a saucepan. Add flour and stir over low heat for 1 minute. Remove from heat, add milk, and stir until smooth.

❷ Return to medium heat and stir continuously until boiling. Lower heat and cook for 3 minutes, stirring frequently. Add salt and pepper.

❸ Add grated cheese and stir until melted. Remove from heat. Beat egg yolks and add.

❹ Beat egg whites until soft peak stage and fold into cheese sauce.

❺ Spoon mixture into a medium-sized ungreased soufflé dish and place in a baking or roasting pan half-filled with water.

❻ Bake in a preheated oven at 180 °C (350 °F/gas 4) for 40–50 minutes. Serve immediately.

Serves 2–4

VARIATIONS

BROCCOLI SOUFFLE

Replace cheese with 315 g (10 oz) cooked and drained broccoli florets added to white sauce.

SWEETCORN SOUFFLE

Add 180 g (6 oz) creamed sweetcorn to basic white sauce.

TIP

Wrap greaseproof paper around the dish to prevent the soufflé from over-flowing. To do this, cut a piece of greaseproof paper long enough to wrap around the dish. Fold it in half, lengthways, butter it to prevent the soufflé from sticking, and tie the paper around the dish with string.

CALZONE

This folded bread, filled with mozzarella cheese, is a delicious variation of a pizza.

1 quantity Pizza Dough (page 14)
90 g (3 oz) rump steak, cut into strips
20 ml (4 tsp) cooking oil
1 onion, chopped
1 courgette, thinly sliced
1 carrot, cut julienne
125 g (4 oz) mozzarella cheese, grated
OR Cheddar cheese
pinch of salt
freshly ground black pepper to taste
5 ml (1 tsp) chopped fresh origano
OR 2.5 ml (½ tsp) dried
beaten egg or milk to glaze

❶ Follow recipe for pizza dough.

❷ After first rising, knock down and divide into two.

❸ Roll out two circles, each about 25 cm (10 inches) in diameter, and 3–5 mm (⅛–¼ inch) thick.

❹ Brown meat in heated oil in a heavy-based saucepan. Add vegetables and stir-fry until cooked but still crisp. Add cheese and seasoning. Place filling on one half of dough, leaving 2.5 cm (1 inch) free around border. Fold dough over and seal edges well.

❺ Place two calzones on a greased baking tray and brush with remaining oil. Cover with cling film and leave to rise in a warm place for about 45 minutes until double in size.

❻ Brush with beaten egg or milk. Bake in a preheated oven at 200 °C (400 °F/ gas 6) for 15–20 minutes, or until golden brown. Serve hot.

Makes 2, depending on size

VARIATION

Substitute any meat of your choice, such as ham or rindless bacon, for steak.

TUNA PIE

60 g (2 oz) margarine
60 ml (4 tbsp) plain flour
340 ml (11 fl oz) milk
2.5 ml (½ tsp) salt
freshly ground black pepper to taste
2 x 200 g (6½ oz) cans solid tuna in vegetable oil, drained and flaked
3 hard-boiled eggs, chopped
1 quantity Shortcrust Pastry (page 30)
beaten egg or milk to glaze

❶ Melt margarine and add flour to make a roux. Add hot milk and boil for a few minutes, stirring continuously until thick.

❷ Add salt, pepper, tuna and chopped eggs. Leave to cool slightly.

❸ Roll out pastry thinly. Line the bottom of a medium-sized, greased ovenproof dish with half the pastry. Fill with tuna filling and cover with remaining pastry. Decorate with pastry strips and brush with beaten egg or milk.

❹ Bake in a preheated oven at 200 °C (400 °F/gas 6) for 20 minutes.

Serves 4

TIP

Canned tuna is always a good store cupboard item. It can be used in fish cakes, salads or pasta sauces.

From top: Cheese Soufflé and Calzone.

3

PASTRIES

PASTRY IS MADE FROM FLOUR, FAT AND LIQUID, AND CAN ALSO INCLUDE SUGAR, EGG YOLKS, OR OTHER INGREDIENTS THAT ENRICH THE PASTRY. THESE BASIC INGREDIENTS ARE THE SAME FOR ALL KINDS OF PASTRY. SHORTCRUST PASTRY REMAINS THE MOST POPULAR AND VERSATILE, WHILE PUFF PASTRY AND FLAKY PASTRY TAKE LONGER TO MAKE AND ARE USED IN SPECIAL DISHES. OTHER PASTRIES THAT ARE BECOMING MORE POPULAR AND ARE VERY VERSATILE ARE CREAM CHEESE AND SODA-WATER PASTRY.

The method for making pastry will depend on the pastry being made, but a few important guidelines for obtaining success are generally applicable and should be followed for best results:

⦿ When making a pastry using wholemeal flour it may be necessary to use less water as the wholemeal absorbs slightly less liquid.

⦿ Always use cold ingredients and equipment, except when making hot-water pastry. The water and fat used for making pastry should be ice-cold.

⦿ Use only butter, as it gives a better result than margarine.

⦿ Use a sharp knife for cutting pastry if no pastry cutter is available.

⦿ Work with your fingertips as they are the coolest part of the hand.

⦿ The amount of liquid specified in a recipe is only a guideline; the amount needed will vary according to the moisture content of the flour used, and the humidity in the atmosphere. Too much liquid will cause the pastry to shrink.

⦿ Do not stretch pastry during preparation as this will cause shrinkage when cooked.

⦿ It is important to work lightly with pastry as overhandling leads to shrinkage.

⦿ Keep your work surface and rolling pin lightly floured. Use a dredger to ensure that flour is spread evenly.

⦿ If possible, roll pastry out on a marble surface as it is cold, smooth and hygienic.

⦿ Never turn pastry over while rolling out.

⦿ Roll pastry in one direction only to maintain an even thickness.

⦿ Leftover pastry should be rolled out and not bundled up.

⦿ Chill pastry in tin before baking to prevent shrinkage in oven.

⦿ Cooking time will depend on thickness and size of case.

⦿ All pastries can be successfully frozen for up to 3 months if stored in an airtight container.

⦿ If frozen, remove pastry from freezer 1 hour prior to use.

Lining a pastry flan

A pastry flan should be carefully lined. If stretched even slightly, the pastry will shrink when baked. After rolling out, lift the pastry gently, with the support of a rolling pin, and place it in the tin. Flour fingertips and press down lightly into base. Allow to stand for 30 minutes before baking.

Baking blind

This involves pre-baking the pastry case before adding the filling. Prick the base, place greaseproof paper over the pastry, and sprinkle with dried beans or peas. Bake according to the recipe, for about 10 minutes. Remove beans. (Store for later use.) Alternatively, use foil, with the shiny side upward. The foil will reflect the heat and prevent the pastry from rising, so the beans are not necessary in this instance. If the pastry case rises to a peak during baking, prick while still soft to allow air to escape.

Sealing edges

This method is used to seal pastry edges, especially when making pies and tarts. To do this, brush one edge with water and press the two edges firmly together. Press lightly on the joined edges using a finger and a knife, gently pinching the edges of the pastry as you go in order to seal them.

Decorating pastries

Your choice of decoration will depend on the type of pastry you are using, and on the size and shape of the dish. Whichever option you choose, start off by sealing the edges neatly.

⦿ Pinch the edge using your forefinger and thumb, or press with a fork.

⦿ Scallop the edge using the blunt edge of a knife.

⦿ Make a fold on the edge of the pastry with your fingers.

⦿ Plait pastry and place around edge.

⦿ Make leaves, hearts, stars or fish. Brush with cold water and place on pastry.

Glazing

Glazing creates an attractive appearance. Glaze savoury dishes by brushing with beaten egg, or milk. Brush sweet pies with egg white; sprinkle with caster sugar.

TYPES OF PASTRY

Shortcrust pastry (Pâte Brisée)

To make shortcrust pastry, use one part fat to two parts flour. Handle the pastry quickly and lightly, using chilled ingredients. Once baked, pastry should be crisp with a fine, even texture.
 Shortcrust pastry becomes hard and tough for one of two reasons: if too much liquid is added, and when pastry is overhandled. Shortcrust pastry dishes include single crust pies, savoury flans, quiches and sweet flans. Remember for the best results: keep ingredients cool, work quickly, and chill pastry in the refrigerator before rolling out.

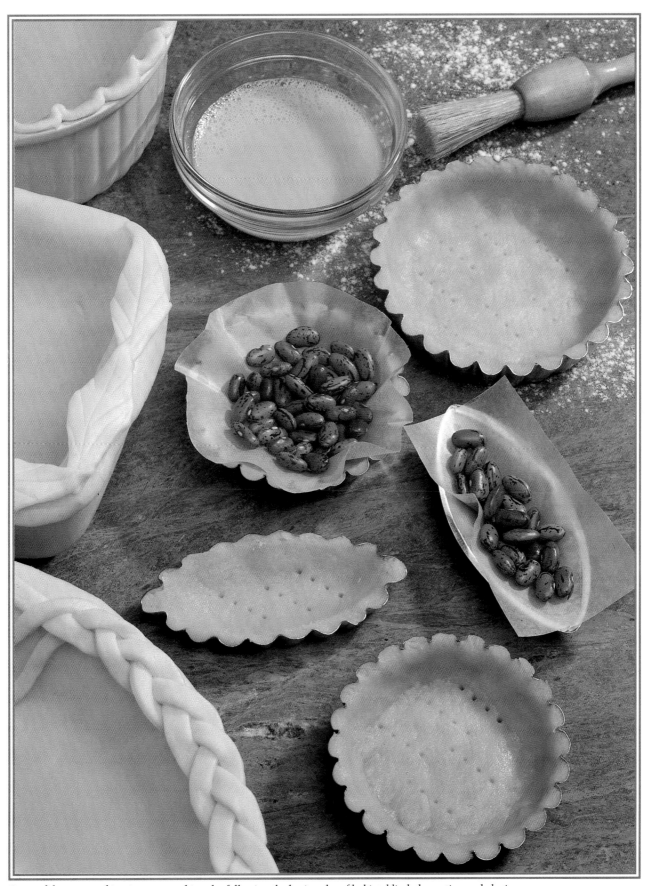

Successful pastry-making is easy to achieve by following the basic rules of baking blind, decorating and glazing.

Rich shortcrust pastry (Pâte Brisée à l'oeuf)

This pastry can be rolled out more thinly than basic shortcrust. Egg yolk and sugar are usually added, resulting in a richer pastry that will stay crisp for longer.

The butter and water used should be cold. Do not overwork the egg and butter, and chill the pastry for at least 30 minutes before rolling out. To line flan tin, lift pastry slightly and slide gently into tin, avoiding stretching. This pastry is ideal for making tartlet shells and is often baked blind.

Sweet flan pastry (Pâte Sucrée)

This pastry is similar to rich shortcrust pastry, with the addition of extra egg, sugar and vanilla extract, and needs a lot of kneading. Refrigerate for at least 30 minutes – a little longer, if possible – before rolling out.

Puff pastry (Pâte Feuilletée)

Its French name meaning 'leafy pastry', puff pastry has a texture that is delicate, very fine and flaky, and is ideal for making pie toppings, fine pastries, tarts, vol-au-vent cases and cocktail snacks.

An equal proportion of fat to flour is used to make this pastry. All ingredients should be well chilled while the pastry is being made and rolled out, and the pastry itself should be chilled a few times to ensure that the layers remain intact. A little lemon juice added to the water will further strengthen the layers.

The pastry rises as follows: the butter between the layers melts during baking and separates the layers, and the water present in the butter turns to steam, which causes the pastry to rise.

When making puff pastry it is essential to keep the ingredients and the work surface cool and to roll the pastry out evenly, without stretching it. Prepare the pastry a day in advance to allow it to rest.

Flaky pastry

This is not as delicate and soft as puff pastry, but it is flaky, rises high, and can be used for the same purposes. It is somewhat easier to make than puff pastry.

Hot-water pastry

The proportion used to make hot-water pastry is roughly one-third fat to flour. It is normally used to make raised pies in special oval, fluted metal pie moulds, and is also used for ham and game pies. Keep pastry warm during preparation and handle it quickly. However, chill before rolling out.

Cream cheese pastry

This rich pastry can be used for savoury or sweet dishes, and is very good if cream or curd cheese is used. It is easy to handle if all the ingredients are cold. Chill well before rolling out.

Soda-water pastry

This is a good substitute for puff pastry as it also has a layered appearance, and is ideal for sweet or savoury dishes. All ingredients should be cold before use.

Choux pastry

This pastry differs from all other pastries because it is made in a saucepan, is soft and should be piped or spooned. When baked, it should be puffed, golden, dry and hollow inside.

For successful results, do not allow the water to boil before the butter has melted, so remove the pan from the heat as soon as the water starts boiling. Add flour all at once, return to heat, and mix until a ball forms. Add eggs one at a time to the slightly cooled mixture. Beat well after each addition.

Choux pastry should be baked until dry to ensure that it holds its shape. The secret, therefore, is to bake it in a very hot oven and then reduce the heat. Turn the heat off and leave the shells in the oven for 10 minutes to ensure that

they dry out. After removing from the oven, pierce each shell to allow the steam to escape.

Fill shells an hour before serving or they will soften. Store empty shells in an airtight container. Heat for a few minutes to crisp up when needed, then fill.

The pastry can be kept in the refrigerator for one day if not needed immediately, or frozen, unbaked, for 3 months.

SHORTCRUST PASTRY

Shortcrust pastry is used for savoury dishes such as pies and pastries. It is suitable for freezing, though not for longer than 3 months.

280 g (9 oz) plain flour
2.5 ml (½ tsp) salt
125 g (4 oz) cold butter
125 ml (4 fl oz) iced water
5 ml (1 tsp) lemon juice or brandy

❶ Sift flour and salt together.

❷ Cut butter into small pieces and rub into flour with fingertips until mixture resembles breadcrumbs.

❸ Mix water and lemon juice into dry ingredients to make a stiff dough. Knead well.

❹ Cover with cling film and refrigerate for 1 hour. Roll out dough on floured surface to a thickness of 3 mm (⅛ inch).

❺ Bake in a preheated oven at 200 °C (400 °F/gas 6) for 20-25 minutes, or until golden brown.

Makes 2 flan cases

VARIATION

Substitute 150 g (5 oz) granary flour for the plain flour.

TIP

The secret of success with this pastry is to avoid using too much liquid, which will make the pastry sticky, resulting in a dry crust. The pastry should be just moistened.

Shortcrust Pastry and Rich Shortcrust Pastry.

RICH SHORTCRUST PASTRY

Enriched by the addition of extra fat, sugar or egg yolk, this pastry is used for sweet and savoury dishes such as pies, pastries, tarts, tartlets or flans, and is also suitable for freezing. When using for savouries, omit the sugar.

280 g (9 oz) plain flour
2.5 ml (½ tsp) salt
180 g (6 oz) cold butter
15 ml (1 tbsp) caster sugar
1 egg yolk
20 ml (4 tsp) iced water
5 ml (1 tsp) lemon juice

❶ Sift flour and salt together.

❷ Cut butter into small pieces and rub into flour with fingertips until mixture resembles breadcrumbs.

❸ Add sugar if using. Mix egg yolk, water and lemon juice into dry ingredients to make a stiff dough. Knead well.

❹ Wrap dough in cling film and chill in refrigerator for about 1 hour. Roll out on a floured surface to a thickness of 3 mm (⅛ inch).

❺ Bake in a preheated oven at 200 °C (400 °F/gas 6) for 20–25 minutes, or until golden brown.

Makes 2 flan cases

<u>VARIATION</u>

Substitute 150 g (5 oz) granary flour for the plain flour.

FLAKY PASTRY

This pastry is not as delicate as puff pastry, but is flaky, rises high, and is easier to make than puff pastry. It has the same applications as puff pastry, namely pie toppings, cream horns and cocktail snacks.

280 g (9 oz) plain flour
2.5 ml (½ tsp) salt
150 g (5 oz) butter
125 ml (4 fl oz) iced water
5 ml (1 tsp) lemon juice

❶ Sift flour and salt together.

❷ Cut butter into pea-sized pieces, add half to flour, and rub in until mixture resembles breadcrumbs.

❸ Mix iced water with lemon juice and cut in with a knife. Mix until smooth, forming a stiff dough.

❹ Flour surface and roll pastry to a thickness of 5 mm (¼ inch), keeping shape rectangular.

❺ Cover two-thirds of pastry with half of remaining butter.

❻ Fold the third of the pastry without butter to meet the other end piece. Fold in thirds again. Keep covered and chill for a while.

❼ Roll out and place remaining butter on two-thirds of pastry, then fold, turn and roll out. Refrigerate for at least 30 minutes.

❽ Bake in a preheated oven at 200 ˚C (400 ˚F/gas 6) for 20–25 minutes, or until golden brown.

SODA-WATER PASTRY

This versatile pastry is delicate and is used for sweet and savoury dishes as well as small pastries such as sausage rolls and cream horns. It can be frozen for up to 3 months.

280 g (9 oz) plain flour
2.5 ml (½ tsp) salt
250 g (8 oz) cold butter
90 ml (6 tbsp) iced soda water
15 ml (1 tbsp) lemon juice or brandy

❶ Sift flour and salt together. Rub in butter with fingertips until mixture resembles breadcrumbs.

❷ Add soda water and lemon juice and mix to a stiff dough.

❸ Wrap in cling film and refrigerate for 1 hour. Roll out dough on a floured surface to a thickness of 3 mm (⅛ inch).

❹ Bake in a preheated oven at 200 ˚C (400 ˚F/gas 6) for 20 minutes, or until golden brown.

PUFF PASTRY

280 g (9 oz) plain flour
2.5 ml (½ tsp) salt
250 g (8 oz) cold butter
125 ml (4 fl oz) iced water
5 ml (1 tsp) lemon juice

❶ Sift flour and salt together. Roll butter into a flat, 15 cm (6 inch) square and keep chilled.

❷ Mix water with lemon juice, pour over flour, and cut in with a knife. Mix until smooth, forming a stiff dough.

❸ Flour surface and roll pastry to a thickness of 5 mm (¼ inch), keeping it rectangular.

❹ Place butter on centre of dough and fold corners to the middle to make an envelope, enclosing butter.

❺ Roll out pastry on a floured surface. Fold into three by turning bottom third up and top third down. Seal edges and chill.

❻ Repeat rolling and folding in three. Chill for 30 minutes.

❼ Repeat rolling and folding pastry seven times, chilling when necessary.

❽ Roll out and refrigerate for at least 30 minutes.

❾ Bake in a preheated oven at 200 ˚C (400 ˚F/gas 6) for 20–25 minutes, or until golden brown.

TIP

Leftover pieces can be rolled out again for later use. Never form into a ball or the layers will be lost.

HOT-WATER PASTRY

Crisp and thicker than usual, this pastry is ideal for the base of pies and is frequently used for pork and game pies.

125 ml (4 fl oz) boiling water
125 g (4 oz) butter or margarine
280 g (9 oz) self-raising flour
2.5 ml (½ tsp) salt

❶ Melt butter in hot water. Sift flour and salt together and mix with liquid until a soft dough is formed.

❷ Refrigerate for 1 hour to cool.

❸ On a floured surface, roll out dough to a thickness of 3 mm (⅛ inch) and bake in a preheated oven at 200 ˚C (400 ˚F/gas 6) for 20 minutes, or until golden brown.

TIP

This is a soft pastry, which should be chilled well before using – for at least 1 hour.

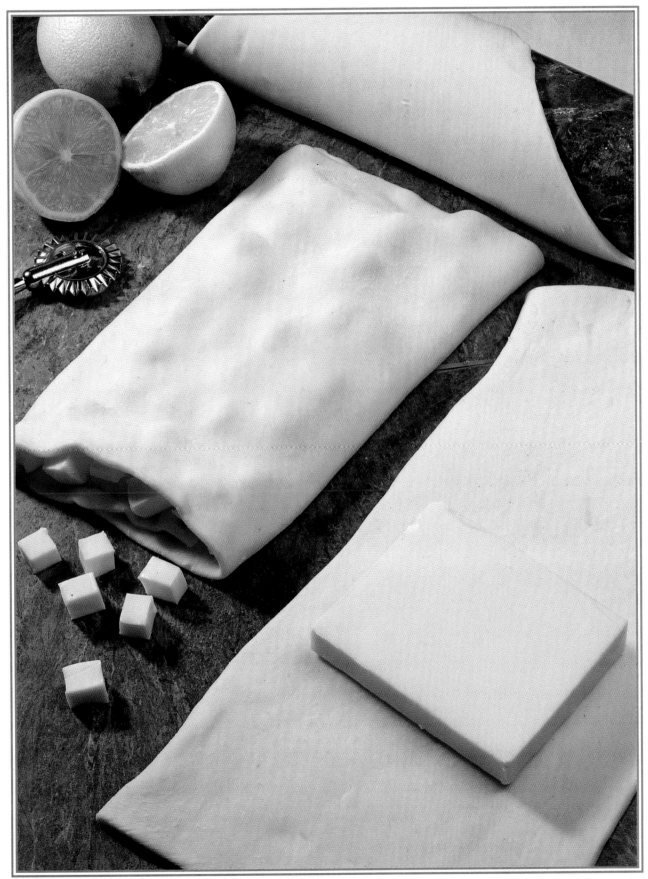

From top: Soda-water Pastry, Puff Pastry and Flaky Pastry.

SWEET FLAN PASTRY

This pastry is used to make delicate sweet tarts. It can be frozen for up to 3 months.

150 g (5 oz) plain flour
2.5 ml (½ tsp) salt
60 ml (4 tbsp) caster sugar
60 g (2 oz) butter
2 egg yolks
2.5 ml (½ tsp) vanilla extract

❶ Sift flour and salt together. Add sugar and rub in butter with fingertips until the mixture resembles fine breadcrumbs.

❷ Add egg yolks and extract and work into a firm dough. Knead pastry well until smooth.

❸ On a floured surface, roll out dough to a thickness of 3 mm (⅛ inch). Line a greased, 23 cm (9 inch) loose-bottomed flan tin.

❹ Cover with cling film; refrigerate for 1 hour. Prick base and bake blind in a preheated oven at 190 °C (375 °F/gas 5) for 10 minutes. Remove paper and beans, then bake a further 5 minutes until pastry is golden brown.

❺ Allow to cool in pan before turning out on to wire rack to cool completely.

Makes one flan case or 12 medium tartlets

VARIATION

Replace half the plain flour with granary flour.

TIP

The food processor is ideal for making this pastry as it needs to be worked thoroughly into a very fine and crisp pastry.

CHOUX PASTRY

This pastry is used for sweet and savoury profiteroles (cream puffs), éclairs or gâteaux. Like other kinds of pastry, it freezes successfully.

125 ml (4 fl oz) water
60 g (2 oz) butter
75 g (2½ oz) plain flour
pinch salt
2 eggs

❶ Place water and butter in a saucepan. Bring slowly to the boil, allowing butter to melt before water boils.

❷ Remove from heat; add flour and salt. Return to heat and stir quickly until a ball forms in the middle, and the dough comes away from the sides.

❸ Remove from heat and leave to cool for about 5 minutes.

❹ Add eggs one at a time, beating well after each addition until dough is stiff.

❺ If making puffs, place teaspoonfuls on greased baking tray or pipe in long shapes for éclairs.

❻ Bake in a preheated oven at 200 °C (400 °F/gas 6) for 10 minutes.

❼ Reduce heat to 180 °C (350 °F/gas 4) for 15 minutes. Leave to cool in oven.

❽ Fill with cream, Confectioner's Custard (page 43) or savoury fillings.

Makes 16 puffs or 12 éclairs

TIPS

Raw dough can be kept, covered, in a cool place for 1 day or frozen for 3 months.

Store empty shells in an airtight container. When needed, reheat for a few minutes to make crisp.

CREAM CHEESE PASTRY

Cream cheese pastry is used for savoury dishes, small pastries and tartlets. It can be frozen for up to 3 months.

150 g (5 oz) plain flour
2.5 ml (½ tsp) salt
125 g (4 oz) cold butter
125 g (4 oz) cream or curd cheese

❶ Sift flour and salt together. Rub in butter until mixture resembles breadcrumbs.

❷ Add cream or curd cheese and mix to a soft dough.

❸ Wrap in cling film and refrigerate for a few hours. On a floured surface, roll out dough to a thickness of 3 mm (⅛ inch).

❹ Bake in a preheated oven at 180 °C (350 °F/gas 4) for 25–30 minutes.

VARIATION

Substitute wholemeal flour for half of the plain flour.

TIPS

To make the pastry easier to work, be sure to have the butter and cream or curd cheese cold. As it is a soft pastry it should be chilled before using.

If pastry has been left overnight in the refrigerator, allow to stand at room temperature for at least 1 hour before rolling out.

From top: Choux Pastry, Sweet Flan Pastry and Cream Cheese Pastry.

WHEN CONSIDERING WHAT TO MAKE FOR TEA, BEAR IN MIND FACTORS LIKE THE AGE OF THE GUESTS AND THE SEASON. SWEET FRUIT TARTS ARE USUALLY A HIT, BUT THE SEASON WILL, TO A LARGE DEGREE, DETERMINE WHAT YOU MAKE. OLD FAVOURITES LIKE SCONES, DOUGHNUTS AND CRUMPETS ARE ALSO IDEAL FOR TEA. FOR SUCCESSFUL TEA PARTIES IT IS ESSENTIAL TO MASTER THE ART OF MAKING RICH SHORTCRUST PASTRY AND SWEET FLAN PASTRY, WHICH WILL ENABLE YOU TO PREPARE DELICIOUS TARTS OR TARTLETS WITH FILLINGS.

SCONES

280 g (9 oz) plain flour
15 ml (1 tbsp) baking powder
2.5 ml (½ tsp) salt
75 ml (5 tbsp) caster sugar
65 g (2 oz) margarine or butter
1 egg
125 ml (4 fl oz) milk

❶ Sift dry ingredients together. Add sugar.

❷ Rub margarine into dry ingredients until mixture resembles breadcrumbs. Mix egg and milk together and add to dry ingredients, forming a soft, but not sticky, dough.

❸ Turn out on to a floured surface and pat out lightly, to a thickness of 2 cm (¾ inch). Cut into rounds or squares. Place on a greased baking tray and bake in a preheated oven at 200 °C (400 °F/gas 6) for 12–15 minutes.

❹ Serve scones with honey, syrup or jam and cream.

Makes about 8, depending on size

VARIATIONS

CHEESE SCONES

Omit sugar and add 125 g (4 oz) grated Cheddar cheese to dry ingredients.

Use celery salt instead of plain salt and omit sugar.

Omit sugar from dough. Pat out and spread with cheese spread, fish paste, sandwich spread or pâté. Roll up dough as for a Swiss roll and cut into 2.5 cm (1 inch) slices. Arrange cut side up on baking trays; bake as usual.

TIP

For delicious, light scones, use half milk and half water.

WHOLEMEAL SCONES

1 egg
60 ml (4 tbsp) cooking oil
about 150 ml (¼ pint) milk
150 g (5 oz) plain flour
150 g (5 oz) granary flour
20 ml (4 tsp) baking powder
2.5 ml (½ tsp) salt

❶ Beat egg lightly with a fork in a 250 ml (8 fl oz) cup, add oil, and fill with milk to 250 ml (8 fl oz) measure.

❷ Sift dry ingredients together. Add bran left behind in sieve.

❸ Make a well in the centre and mix in the liquid. Mix to a soft dough.

❹ Turn out on to a floured surface, pat lightly to a thickness of 2 cm (¾ inch) and cut into rounds with a pastry cutter.

❺ Place scones on a greased baking tray and bake in a preheated oven at 220 °C (425 °F/gas 7) for 10–15 minutes.

Makes about 8, depending on size

VARIATIONS

FRUIT SCONES

Add 75 g (2½ oz) mixed dried fruit or 45 g (1½ oz) chopped, stewed fruit, and 15 ml (1 tbsp) caster sugar to dry ingredients.

CHEESE SCONES

Add 125 g (4 oz) grated Cheddar cheese and a pinch of cayenne pepper to wholemeal scone recipe.

For breakfast, make one large scone.

TIP

Freeze scones for up to 6 months in an airtight container or wrapping.

CRUMPETS

150 g (5 oz) plain flour
10 ml (2 tsp) baking powder
pinch of salt
30 ml (2 tbsp) sugar
1 egg
200 ml (6½ fl oz) milk
15 ml (1 tbsp) melted margarine

❶ Sift flour, baking powder and salt together. Add sugar.

❷ Beat the egg, milk and melted margarine together and add to dry ingredients.

❸ Beat until smooth and leave to stand for 30 minutes.

❹ Fry spoonfuls of batter on a hot, greased griddle or frying pan.

❺ Fry until golden brown, turning when bubbles appear on surface.

❻ Serve with butter, jam or honey.

Makes 12–15

TIPS

After removing crumpets from griddle, place on a clean, dry tea-towel to keep soft.

Freeze crumpets on top of one another, wrapping a few together in cling film. Keep in deep-freeze for up to 2 months.

From top: Wholemeal Scones and Scones.

CHEESY BROWN CRUMPETS

210 g (7 oz) brown bread flour
10 ml (2 tsp) baking powder
pinch salt
125 g (4 oz) Cheddar cheese, grated
125 ml (4 fl oz) cooking oil
125 ml (4 fl oz) milk
3 eggs
45 ml (3 tbsp) sugar

❶ Sift brown bread flour, baking powder and salt together, and add cheese. Add bran left behind in sieve.

❷ Beat oil, milk, eggs and sugar together until sugar has dissolved. Mix with dry ingredients to form a smooth batter.

❸ Allow to stand for 30 minutes before frying spoonfuls on a hot, greased griddle or in a frying pan. When bubbles appear on surface, turn crumpets and allow to fry on the other side. Repeat until all the batter has been used.

❹ Serve hot with butter or margarine.

Makes 20

TIP

Always mix liquid into flour, and not the other way around. If lumps form, rub mixture through a sieve. Batter should have the consistency of thin cream.

DOUGHNUTS

280 g (9 oz) plain flour
5 ml (1 tsp) salt
7.5 ml (1½ tsp) instant dry yeast
30 g (1 oz) butter or margarine
1 egg, beaten
150 ml (¼ pint) warm milk
sieved apricot jam
cooking oil for frying
caster sugar

❶ Sift the flour and salt together and add yeast.

❷ Rub in butter until mixture resembles fine breadcrumbs.

❸ Combine egg and milk. Add to dry ingredients, mixing to a soft dough.

❹ Knead for about 10 minutes, until dough is smooth and elastic.

❺ Place dough in an oiled bowl, cover, and allow to rest for about 30 minutes.

❻ Knock down and divide into 12 pieces.

❼ Roll into balls and make a hole in the middle of each with your finger. Fill with about one teaspoon jam and pinch closed.

❽ Cover with oiled cling film and allow to rise in a warm place until double in size – about 20 minutes.

❾ Deep-fry in hot oil until golden brown.

❿ Drain on paper towels and toss in caster sugar.

Makes 20

VARIATION

Fry the doughnuts first, make a hole in the centre of each with your finger, and then fill with jam.

TIP

To make ring doughnuts, cut out rounds from centre. Fry small rounds, too, and coat both with glacé icing or melted chocolate.

WAFFLES

210 g (7 oz) plain flour
15 ml (1 tbsp) baking powder
2.5 ml (½ tsp) salt
15 ml (1 tbsp) sugar
315 ml (½ pint) milk
2 eggs, separated
45 g (1½ oz) butter, melted, or cooking oil

❶ Sift dry ingredients. Add sugar.

❷ Whisk milk, egg yolks and melted butter together. Add to dry ingredients, mixing until smooth.

❸ Fold in beaten egg whites and leave batter to stand for 30 minutes.

❹ Bake in a hot waffle pan until waffle is golden brown. Serve warm with syrup, honey or Caramel Sauce.

Makes 6 waffles, depending on size

TIP

If the waffle pan is too cold the waffles will stick, or be spotted. A moderately hot temperature is ideal and has been reached when a few drops of cold water sprinkled on the heated grid form bouncy white balls.

Caramel sauce

180 g (6 oz) soft brown sugar
45 g (1½ oz) butter
250 ml (8 fl oz) milk
25 ml (5 tsp) custard powder
pinch salt
5 ml (1 tsp) caramel extract

❶ Caramelize brown sugar and butter slightly until they start to brown.

❷ Remove from heat; gradually add 200 ml (6½ fl oz) heated milk. Stir to dissolve sugar.

❸ Mix custard powder, salt and remaining milk to a smooth paste.

❹ Add to milk and bring to boil until thick, then cook for about 3 minutes.

❺ Remove from heat and add extract.

TIP

For a thicker sauce, add more custard powder.

From top: Doughnuts, Cheesy Brown Crumpets and Waffles.

STRAWBERRY CHIFFON TART

15 ml (1 tbsp) gelatine
60 ml (4 tbsp) cold water
2 eggs, separated
15 ml (1 tbsp) lemon juice
125 g (4 oz) caster sugar
250 ml (8 fl oz) crushed fresh strawberries

1 quantity Sweet Flan Pastry, baked (page 34)

❶ Soak gelatine in the cold water and dissolve over hot water.

❷ Beat egg yolks slightly, add lemon juice and 90 ml (6 tbsp) of sugar. Cook in top of double boiler over simmering water, stirring constantly until thickened.

❸ Remove from heat and stir in gelatine until dissolved. Add strawberries and chill mixture until it starts to thicken.

❹ Beat egg whites with remaining sugar until soft peak stage. Fold into strawberry mixture.

❺ Fill baked pastry shell, chill until set, and garnish with strawberries and whipped cream.

TIPS

Beat egg whites until they are stiff, but not too dry.

To test whether the gelatine has begun to set, place a spoon into the mixture, and then remove the spoon. If the gelatine has started to set, the mixture should stay apart for a few seconds.

PUFFY APPLE RINGS

150 g (5 oz) self-raising flour
2.5 ml (½ tsp) salt
1 egg, separated
200 ml (6½ fl oz) milk
3 apples, peeled and cored
cooking oil for frying
cinnamon sugar

❶ Sift flour and salt together. Beat in egg yolk and milk until smooth.

❷ Beat egg white until soft peak stage and fold gently into batter.

❸ Slice apples into rings about 5 mm (¼ inch) thick, cover with batter and deep-fry in hot oil.

❹ Drain apple rings on paper towels and sprinkle with cinnamon sugar. Eat immediately as they become soggy quickly.

Makes about 15

TIP

Cooking oil is ready for frying when it turns a cube of bread pale brown in about 45 seconds.

LEMON MERINGUE PIE

400 g (13 oz) can condensed milk
125 ml (4 fl oz) lemon juice
5 ml (1 tsp) grated lemon rind
2 eggs, separated
1 quantity Sweet Flan Pastry, baked (page 34)
25 ml (5 tsp) caster sugar

❶ Combine condensed milk, lemon juice, lemon rind and egg yolks and mix well until smooth.

❷ Spoon into baked pastry shell.

❸ Beat egg whites and gradually add caster sugar while beating, until soft peak stage.

❹ Cover filling with meringue and bake in a preheated oven at 180 °C (350 °F/gas 4) for about 10 minutes, or until golden brown. Remember that meringue burns easily.

TIPS

One average lemon yields about 45 ml (3 tbsp) juice.

Cut a meringue neatly using a knife blade that has been lightly coated in cooking oil.

BANANA FRITTERS

150 g (5 oz) plain flour
10 ml (2 tsp) baking powder
15 ml (1 tbsp) cornflour
2.5 ml (½ tsp) salt
1 egg
125 ml (4 fl oz) milk
45 ml (3 tbsp) sugar
15 ml (1 tbsp) cooking oil
4 bananas, halved and then quartered
cooking oil for frying
cinnamon
caster sugar

❶ Sift flour, baking powder, cornflour and salt together.

❷ Whisk egg, milk, sugar and oil together and add to dry ingredients. Mix until smooth and leave to stand for 30 minutes.

❸ Dip banana pieces into batter and deep-fry in hot oil until golden brown.

❹ Drain on paper towels and sprinkle with cinnamon and caster sugar.

Makes 16

VARIATION

Substitute any other fruit, such as pineapple or cherries, for bananas.

TIPS

Squeeze lemon juice over raw, peeled apples or bananas to prevent discoloration.

To deep-fry fritters, use an electric fryer, deep-frying pan or deep, wide saucepan. Pour in cooking oil to a depth of at least 7.5 cm (3 inches).

To shallow-fry fritters, use a heavy frying pan and pour in cooking oil to a depth of not more than 5 mm (¼ inch).

From top: Strawberry Chiffon Pie, Puffy Apple Rings, Banana Fritters and Lemon Meringue Pie.

APPLE TART

FILLING
3 large green apples, peeled, cored and sliced OR 375 g (12 oz) can pie apples
125 g (4 oz) sugar
90 g (3 oz) raisins
5 ml (1 tsp) ground cinnamon
4 cloves
20 ml (4 tsp) lemon juice

BASE AND CRUST
125 g (4 oz) margarine
125 g (4 oz) caster sugar
1 egg
280 g (9 oz) plain flour
10 ml (2 tsp) baking powder
2.5 ml (½ tsp) salt

❶ For filling: Mix apple slices with other filling ingredients in a saucepan.

❷ Simmer for about 5 minutes. Drain off excess juice and leave to cool. Remove cloves.

❸ For base and crust: Beat margarine and sugar together. Add egg and beat until light and fluffy.

❹ Sift dry ingredients and add to egg mixture, forming a soft dough.

❺ Press half of dough into a greased 23 cm (9 inch) pie dish. Spoon apple filling onto pastry.

❻ Coarsely grate remaining dough over filling.

❼ Bake in a preheated oven at 160 °C (325 °F/gas 3) for 1 hour.

❽ Dust with icing sugar and serve hot or cold with cream.

TIP

To prevent a soggy base, sprinkle bottom of pastry with a mixture of flour and sugar before placing fruit on top.

FRUIT CUSTARD TARTLETS

1 quantity Sweet Flan Pastry (page 34) OR Rich Shortcrust Pastry (page 30) baked blind in tartlet tins

FILLING
250 ml (8 fl oz) milk
45 ml (3 tbsp) caster sugar
45 ml (3 tbsp) cornflour
pinch salt
1 egg
5 ml (1 tsp) vanilla extract or lemon juice
250 ml (8 fl oz) cream, whipped

TOPPING
500 g (1 lb) fresh fruit such as strawberries, sliced bananas, pitted cherries, mandarin segments, sliced peaches, skinned grapes, blueberries, gooseberries, sliced pawpaw

GLAZE
165 g (5½ oz) sieved apricot jam
15 ml (1 tbsp) water, brandy or lemon juice

❶ For filling: Heat milk in a saucepan. Mix sugar, cornflour and salt with a little of the milk. Add to remaining milk and bring to boil, stirring constantly until mixture starts to thicken.

❷ Beat egg slightly. Add some of warm mixture and return to saucepan; cook for a few minutes while beating to prevent lumps from forming.

❸ Cool, add extract and whipped cream. Fill tartlet cases.

❹ For topping: Arrange fruit on filling.

❺ For glaze: Heat ingredients together, stirring until smooth. Brush fruit with warm glaze.

Makes 12–15, depending on size

VARIATION

PASSION FRUIT TARTLETS

Substitute passion fruit sauce for fruit topping.

110 g (3½ oz) can passion fruit pulp
10 ml (2 tsp) lemon juice
375 g (12 oz) icing sugar
Mix all ingredients until smooth.

BRANDY SNAPS

125 g (4 oz) butter
125 g (4 oz) sugar
180 g (6 oz) golden syrup
150 g (5 oz) plain flour
2.5 ml (½ tsp) salt
5 ml (1 tsp) ground ginger
15 ml (1 tbsp) brandy
500 ml (16 fl oz) cream, whipped

❶ Place butter, sugar and syrup in a heavy-based saucepan; stir over moderate heat until sugar has dissolved. Remove from heat and cool slightly.

❷ Stir flour, salt and ginger into mixture. Stir well and add brandy.

❸ Drop teaspoonfuls of mixture onto greased baking tray, allowing enough space for spreading.

❹ Bake in a preheated oven at 180 °C (350 °F/gas 4) for 10–12 minutes. Remove with buttered spatula and roll around the greased handle of a wooden spoon. Leave a few minutes until biscuit firms.

❺ Store in an airtight container for a few days and fill with whipped cream, spooned or piped in.

Makes 40

VARIATION

Cool brandy snaps flat; serve layered with whipped cream and strawberries.

TIPS

Use the entire blade of the spatula and not only the point to lift the freshly cooked brandy snaps.

Do not bake longer than 10–12 minutes or snaps will be tough, not crisp.

After baking: Turn off the heat and open the oven door, leaving the biscuits in the oven to keep warm while you work. If allowed to cool they will become hard and brittle and impossible to shape – so work quickly! If biscuits begin hardening before moulding, return to oven at 140 °C (275 °F/gas 1) for a minute or two until they soften ·

From top: Apple Tart, Brandy Snaps, Fruit Custard Tartlets and Custard Slice.

CUSTARD SLICES

CONFECTIONER'S CUSTARD
375 ml (12 fl oz) milk
75 ml (5 tbsp) sugar
30 ml (2 tbsp) plain flour
20 ml (4 tsp) cornflour
2 eggs
2 egg yolks
2.5 ml (½ tsp) vanilla extract

1 quantity Puff Pastry (page 32) OR
1 quantity Flaky Pastry (page 32)
Glacé Icing (page 67)

❶ Bring 315 ml (½ pint) milk to the boil. Mix sugar, flour and cornflour with remaining milk.

❷ Add hot milk to flour paste. Beat eggs and egg yolks, and gradually add to the warm mixture.

❸ Return to hob and cook over low heat, stirring constantly until thickened. Leave to cool before adding vanilla extract.

❹ Roll out pastry and cut into 10 x 5 cm (4 x 2 inches) rectangles. Bake in a preheated oven at 200 °C (400 °F/gas 6) for 15 minutes, until golden brown.

❺ Spread custard on half of the pastry pieces. Place remaining pastry pieces on top and decorate with Glacé Icing (page 67).

Makes 16–20

VARIATION

Sandwich the pastry slices together with strawberry jam and cream.

TIP

Keep refrigerated for up to 2 days.

CREAM PUFFS

**1 quantity Choux Pastry (page 34)
fresh cream, beaten
cooking chocolate, melted OR
icing sugar**

❶ To make puffs, place teaspoonfuls of pastry on greased baking tray.

❷ Bake in a preheated oven at 200 °C (400 °F/gas 6) for 10 minutes and reduce to 180 °C (350 °F/gas 4) for 15 minutes.

❸ When cool, fill with cream and top with melted chocolate or dust with icing sugar. Alternatively, fill with Lemon Filling, Ham and Cheese Filling or Custard Filling (all this page).

Makes 16

VARIATIONS

ECLAIRS

Spoon choux pastry into a piping bag and pipe onto éclair tin. Spoon melted chocolate or Chocolate Glacé Icing (page 58) over baked éclair, once cool.

Makes 12

Savoury puffs are made a little smaller. Fill just before serving or pastry will become soft.

For a quick dessert: fill puffs with spoonfuls of cream or ice cream and pour hot, melted chocolate over. To melt chocolate: Chocolate should never be melted over direct heat or come into contact with water. Instead, use a double boiler, placing the chocolate in a pot over boiling water. The water in the bottom pot should not touch the base of the top saucepan. Bring the water to the boil, stirring chocolate until smooth. For melting chocolate in the microwave, set power on High or 100 % for 2–3 minutes; cook until chocolate has melted, stirring once.

Lemon Filling

**125 ml (4 fl oz) boiling water
5 ml (1 tsp) grated lemon rind
90 g (3 oz) sugar
30 ml (2 tbsp) cornflour
1 egg, beaten
45 ml (3 tbsp) lemon juice
15 ml (½ oz) margarine**

❶ Mix boiling water and lemon rind together.

❷ Add to dry ingredients in a saucepan. Boil until mixture has thickened.

❸ Pour some of the hot mixture onto beaten egg, then add this to rest of hot mixture. Add lemon juice and margarine.

Ham and Cheese Filling

**30 g (1 oz) margarine
30 ml (2 tbsp) plain flour
250 ml (8 fl oz) milk
2.5 ml (½ tsp) salt
pinch cayenne pepper
15 ml (1 tbsp) chopped fresh parsley OR
5 ml (1 tsp) dried
100 g (3 oz) smoked ham, chopped
125 g (4 oz) Cheddar cheese, grated**

❶ Heat margarine in a saucepan and add flour. Add hot milk and stir constantly while cooking until thickened. Add salt, cayenne pepper and parsley.

❷ Add ham and cheese and leave mixture to cool before using.

Custard Filling

**75 g (2½ oz) plain flour
125 g (4 oz) sugar
2.5 ml (½ tsp) salt
500 ml (16 fl oz) milk
2 eggs, beaten
15 g (½ oz) butter
5 ml (1 tsp) vanilla extract**

❶ Mix flour, sugar and salt in the top of a double boiler. Add milk and beat until smooth.

❷ Pour a little hot milk mixture into beaten eggs; return this to rest of hot custard mixture.

❸ Beat while cooking until thickened, – about 3 minutes. Remove from heat and add butter and vanilla extract. Leave to cool.

VARIATION

Substitute lemon extract for vanilla extract.

CREAM HORNS

**1 quantity Puff Pastry (page 32) OR
Flaky Pastry (page 32)
1 egg white, beaten
60 ml (4 tbsp) strawberry jam
125 ml (4 fl oz) whipping cream**

❶ Roll out pastry into a rectangular shape, to a thickness of 3 mm (⅛ inch). Cut into strips 2.5 cm (1 inch) wide. Brush these lightly with beaten egg white.

❷ Grease cream horn moulds and, with damp side inwards, turn strips around greased moulds, starting at the pointed end of the mould and making sure that the strips overlap.

❸ Brush with egg white and place on a greased baking tray.

❹ Bake in a preheated oven at 220 °C (425 °F/gas 7) for 8–10 minutes, until crisp and golden brown. Allow to cool.

❺ Place 5 ml (1 tsp) jam inside and fill with beaten cream.

Makes 12

TIP

Pastry horns lose their crispness very quickly. To ensure crispness, do not make them more than 2 hours before needed. Fill at the last minute.

From top: Puffs with Ham and Cheese Filling and Cream Horns.

BASIC FLAN

60 g (2 oz) butter
125 ml (4 fl oz) milk
2 eggs
200 g (6½ oz) sugar
210 g (7 oz) plain flour
10 ml (2 tsp) baking powder
pinch salt

❶ Heat butter and milk together until butter has melted.

❷ Beat eggs and sugar until light and fluffy.

❸ Sift dry ingredients and fold into egg mixture, together with milk. Beat slightly until smooth.

❹ Pour into two greased, fluted 23 cm (9 inch) flan tins. Bake in a preheated oven at 180 °C (350 °F/gas 4) for 15–20 minutes.

❺ Leave flans in tins for a few minutes before turning on to a wire rack to cool.

❻ Fill with Ginger Filling, Gooseberry and Orange Filling or Pineapple Filling (all this page).

Makes 2 flans

TIP

If kept airtight, flans can be success-fully frozen for 4–5 months.

Ginger Filling

250 ml (8 fl oz) water
250 ml (8 fl oz) golden syrup
45 ml (3 tbsp) custard powder
2.5 ml (½ tsp) ground ginger
whipped cream for decorating

❶ Bring 200 ml (6½ fl oz) water and the syrup to boil. Dissolve custard powder in remaining water.

❷ Pour warm syrup into custard powder, add ginger and pour back into saucepan.

❸ Boil until thickened – about 3 minutes.

❹ Leave to cool slightly and then pour into flan.

❺ When set, decorate with cream.

Gooseberry and Orange Filling

410 g (13 oz) can gooseberries in syrup
180 g (6 oz) golden syrup
90 ml (6 tbsp) orange juice
45 ml (3 tbsp) custard powder
5 ml (1 tsp) grated orange rind
whipped cream for decorating

❶ Drain gooseberries and pour syrup into saucepan. Bring to boil.

❷ Stir in golden syrup and reheat until boiling.

❸ Mix orange juice and custard powder together to a smooth paste. Stir into syrup mixture. Cook until mixture is smooth and thickened.

❹ Add gooseberries and orange rind. Leave mixture to cool slightly, then pour into flan. Chill in refrigerator for a while to set.

❺ Decorate with cream.

Pineapple Filling

15 g (½ oz) margarine
200 g (6½ oz) sugar
1 egg, separated
25 ml (5 tsp) cornflour
165 g (5½ oz) crushed pineapple
2.5 ml (½ tsp) salt
2.5 ml (½ tsp) vanilla extract
125 ml (4 fl oz) cream, whipped

❶ Cook margarine, sugar, egg yolk, cornflour and pineapple together until thickened.

❷ Add salt, vanilla extract, beaten egg white and whipped cream. Leave mixture to cool before filling prepared flan case.

CRUSTLESS MILK TART

30 g (1 oz) butter
4 eggs, separated
250 g (8 oz) caster sugar
150 g (5 oz) plain flour
5 ml (1 tsp) baking powder
pinch salt
1 litre (1¾ pints) milk
5 ml (1 tsp) vanilla extract
ground cinnamon

❶ Melt butter. Add egg yolks and caster sugar, and beat well.

❷ Sift dry ingredients together and add to egg yolk mixture.

❸ Beat in milk and extract. Fold in beaten egg whites, then pour mixture into a greased 23 x 33 cm (9 x 13 inch) ovenproof tart dish.

❹ Sprinkle with cinnamon and bake in a preheated oven at 180 °C (350 °F/gas 4) for 55–60 minutes.

TIP

To separate the yolk of an egg from the white, break the egg into a saucer, upturn a small glass over the yolk, and pour off the white.

PECAN PIE

½ quantity Rich Shortcrust Pastry (page 31)
125 g (4 oz) pecan nuts
60 g (2 oz) butter, melted
125 g (4 oz) soft brown sugar
3 eggs, beaten
90 ml (6 tbsp) golden syrup
5 ml (1 tsp) vanilla extract

❶ Roll out pastry and line a greased 23 cm (9 inch) pie dish. Bake blind in a preheated oven at 180 °C (350 °F/gas 4) for 10 minutes. Remove paper and beans.

❷ Arrange pecan nuts over partially cooked pastry case.

❸ Lightly beat melted butter, sugar and eggs together. Add syrup while beating until foamy. Add extract.

❹ Pour egg mixture over nuts. Bake in a preheated oven at 180 °C (350 °F/gas 4) for 40–45 minutes. Leave to set.

❺ Serve hot or cold with whipped cream or ice cream.

TIP

After baking, pie will not be quite set, but will set once slightly cooled.

From top: Pecan Pie and Basic Flan with Gooseberry and Orange Filling.

5

CAKES

A BIRTHDAY PARTY OR SPECIAL TEA PARTY IS INCOMPLETE WITHOUT A CAKE. INCLUDING SOMETHING FOR EVERY OCCASION, THIS CHAPTER OFFERS A DELICIOUS SELECTION OF OLD FAVOURITES AND NEW IDEAS THAT WILL SUIT A VARIETY OF TASTES – AND BUDGETS!
PLAIN CAKES CAN BE TRANSFORMED INTO SPECIAL TREATS WITH FILLINGS OR TOPPINGS TO SUIT THE OCCASION. EXPERIENCED AND INEXPERIENCED BAKERS ALIKE WILL HAVE GREAT SUCCESS WITH ANY OF THESE IRRESISTIBLE CAKES.

GUIDELINES FOR BAKING CAKES

Preparing and mixing

To ensure success when baking cakes it is essential to weigh and measure accurately, and to follow the recipe carefully. Use the minimum amount of liquid, as more can always be added if necessary.

Using an electric mixer is much easier and quicker than beating by hand. Start on low speed and, once the ingredients are combined, increase speed. Avoid overbeating as this breaks down the air bubbles that have formed in the mixture.

Bake the cake as soon after mixing as possible as, after standing too long, it may not rise as it should. Bang tin slightly before baking to remove air bubbles.

It is important to use the recommended tin size as the baking time will be different for other tin sizes. Baking times provided in the recipes are approximate, however, because many factors may influence the time required.

All of the recipes in this book have been tested in a conventional oven; a microwave oven was not used as cooking times differ too much. For baking, conventional ovens produce better results.

Greasing cake tins

Most cake tins – even the 'non-stick' ones – need greasing. This can be done by brushing, spreading or spraying oil or fat over the inside of the tin.

Lining cake tins

For cakes that are moist and break easily, it will be necessary to line the tin. Heavy fruit cakes need a few layers of lining to prevent the cake from browning too much.

Use the base of the tin as a guideline for cutting out a circle of greaseproof paper. The circle should be 5 cm (2 inches) larger as it should be snipped at intervals. The lining for the sides should also be cut 5 cm (2 inches) larger. Place the lining for the sides in the tin first, and then the base lining.

Flouring cake tins

Flour is sometimes dusted lightly on the inside of the tin after greasing to give extra protection against sticking. Sprinkle flour sparingly over the greased surface and shake off excess.

Testing cakes

Only start testing your cake after three-quarters of the baking time has been completed, using one of the following methods:

● Press the top of the cake lightly. If the cake is done, it will spring back and no impression will be left. This is a good way of testing if lighter cakes are cooked.

● Insert a fine skewer into the centre of the cake, then remove. If the cake is cooked, no cake mixture should stick to the skewer.

● When ready, the cake will come away from the sides of the tin.

Cooling

Allow cakes to settle in the tin for 5–10 minutes before turning out and cooling on a wire rack. Air can then circulate and prevent the cake from becoming soggy.

To prevent wire rack marks from forming on the cake during cooling, place a clean tea towel on the rack before turning the cake on to it. Do not ice cakes until they are completely cold.

Storing

Cakes are best stored in an airtight container in a cool place. A piece of apple placed in the container helps to keep cakes moist.

Cream cakes or vegetable cakes should be stored in the refrigerator. Store sponge cakes and quick mixes for 2–4 days; rich fruit cakes 4–6 months.

Freezing

Unfilled and undecorated cakes freeze well for 3–6 months. Cakes can be frozen while still slightly warm to ensure greater freshness after defrosting.

To freeze, wrap cake in cling film or heavy foil, making sure that it is airtight, and freeze as quickly as possible to prevent the formation of ice crystals.

Sometimes it is more convenient to freeze cakes when they have been filled and iced. The best fillings and icings for freezing are those with a high fat content. Water icing will be brittle on thawing. Place iced cakes in the freezer, uncovered, until firm. Remove from freezer, wrap and seal, then return to freezer. Iced cakes freeze well and will last for up to 3 months.

Defrosting

Undecorated cakes to defrost at room temperature for 1–2 hours, depending on size; then fill and decorate. Decorated cakes should be thawed in the refrigerator overnight. Defrosting can also be done in a microwave, but the cake will become stale more quickly.

Baking and cooling cakes.

CARROT AND BANANA CAKE

90 g (3 oz) soft brown sugar
2 eggs
125 ml (4 fl oz) cooking oil
150 g (5 oz) white bread flour
10 ml (2 tsp) baking powder
5 ml (1 tsp) bicarbonate of soda
125 g (4 oz) carrots, finely grated
3 large bananas, mashed
90 g (3 oz) seedless raisins or sultanas
icing sugar

❶ Whisk sugar, eggs and oil together.

❷ Sift dry ingredients and add, alternately with carrot, bananas and raisins, to egg mixture.

❸ Pour the mixture into a greased 23 cm (9 inch) ring cake tin. Bake in a preheated oven at 180 °C (350 °F/gas 4) for 35–40 minutes.

❹ Leave in tin for a few minutes before turning on to a wire rack to cool. Dust with icing sugar.

TIP

If baked in a ring tin, the cake will be much easier to slice and serve.

NUTTY CHERRY CAKE

125 g (4 oz) margarine
90 g (3 oz) soft brown sugar
2 eggs, separated
210 g (7 oz) plain flour
2.5 ml (½ tsp) salt
5 ml (1 tsp) baking powder
90 ml (6 tbsp) milk

TOPPING
180 g (6 oz) glacé cherries, halved
90 g (3 oz) pecan nuts, chopped
75 ml (5 tbsp) icing sugar

❶ Beat margarine and sugar together until light and creamy.

❷ Add egg yolks one at a time, beating well after each addition.

❸ Sift dry ingredients and add alternately with milk to creamed egg mixture.

❹ Spread batter evenly into a greased, loose-bottomed 20 cm (8 inch) round cake tin.

❺ For topping: Beat egg whites until soft peak stage.

❻ Fold cherries, nuts and icing sugar into egg whites.

❼ Spread on top of batter and bake in a preheated oven at 160 °C (325 °F/gas 3) for 1¼ hours.

TIPS

If you notice that the meringue is browning too quickly, reduce the oven temperature.

Do not turn cake out to cool; instead, leave on cake tin base and place on wire rack.

CHOCOLATE OIL CAKE

4 eggs
250 g (8 oz) granulated sugar
210 g (7 oz) plain flour
45 ml (3 tbsp) cocoa powder
15 ml (1 tbsp) baking powder
2.5 ml (½ tsp) salt
125 ml (4 fl oz) boiling water
125 ml (4 fl oz) cooking oil
grated chocolate

CHOCOLATE BUTTER ICING
125 g (4 oz) butter
375 g (12 oz) icing sugar
30 ml (2 tbsp) cocoa powder
5 ml (1 tsp) vanilla extract

❶ Whisk the eggs and sugar together until light and fluffy.

❷ Sift dry ingredients and gently fold into mixture with water and oil.

❸ Turn into two lined, greased 20 cm (8 inch) cake tins and bake in a pre-heated oven at 180 °C (350 °F/gas 4) for 20–25 minutes. Leave for a few minutes in tins before turning out on to a wire rack to continue cooling.

❹ For icing: Beat all ingredients together until smooth and creamy.

❺ Sandwich and top cake with icing. Decorate with grated chocolate.

VARIATIONS

Add 10 ml (2 tsp) grated orange rind to dry ingredients and 5 ml (1 tsp) grated orange rind to chocolate icing.

Add 2.5 ml (½ tsp) ground cinnamon and 5 ml (1 tsp) instant coffee to dry ingredients.

Add 5 ml (1 tsp) peppermint extract to ingredients and 2.5 ml (½ tsp) to chocolate icing.

ORANGE FRUIT RING

125 g (4 oz) margarine
250 g (8 oz) sugar
2 eggs
280 g (9 oz) plain flour
5 ml (1 tsp) baking powder
150 g (5 oz) mixed dried fruit
10 ml (2 tsp) orange rind, grated
5 ml (1 tsp) bicarbonate of soda
250 ml (8 fl oz) soured milk

SYRUP
125 g (4 oz) sugar
125 ml (4 fl oz) orange juice
30 ml (2 tbsp) lemon juice
5 ml (1 tsp) grated orange rind

❶ Cream margarine and sugar together. Add eggs and beat well until light and fluffy.

❷ Sift flour and baking powder and add to creamed mixture. Add dried fruit and orange rind.

❸ Dissolve bicarbonate of soda in soured milk and add to mixture.

❹ Lightly grease a 23 cm (9 inch) ring cake tin and bake in a preheated oven at 180 °C (350 °F/gas 4) for 45–50 minutes.

❺ For syrup: Mix ingredients together and boil for 2 minutes.

❻ Remove cake from oven and spoon syrup over hot cake.

TIP

When grating rind from oranges or lemons, do not grate the pith as it will give a bitter taste.

Clockwise from top: Orange Fruit Ring, Chocolate Oil Cake, Nutty Cherry Cake and Carrot and Banana Cake.

CARROT CAKE

4 eggs
375 g (12 oz) caster sugar
250 ml (8 fl oz) cooking oil
280 g (9 oz) plain flour
10 ml (2 tsp) baking powder
2.5 ml (½ tsp) salt
5 ml (1 tsp) ground cinnamon
2.5 ml (½ tsp) ground ginger
2.5 ml (½ tsp) ground cloves
2.5 ml (½ tsp) bicarbonate of soda
375 g (12 oz) carrots, finely grated
90 g (3 oz) seedless raisins
**60 g (2 oz) pecan nuts, chopped,
optional**

SOFT CHEESE ICING
110 g (3½ oz) butter or margarine
125 g (4 oz) curd cheese
500 g (1 lb) icing sugar
10 ml (2 tsp) lemon juice

❶ Whisk eggs and sugar together until light and fluffy.

❷ Add oil and beat well.

❸ Sift dry ingredients together and add to beaten mixture. Fold in carrot, raisins and nuts.

❹ Pour mixture into two lined and greased 20 cm (8 inch) cake tins.

❺ Bake in a preheated oven at 180 °C (350 °F/gas 4) for 35–40 minutes. Leave in the tin for a few minutes after removing from oven, before turning out on to a wire rack to continue cooling.

❻ For icing: Combine all ingredients and mix until smooth.

❼ Spread icing on cooled cake.

TIP

As the layers are large, they can be iced individually, resulting in two separate cakes.

LOW-FAT CHEESECAKE

**20 cm (8 inch) sponge cake layer
(page 57)
25 ml (5 tsp) gelatine
100 ml (3½ fl oz) water
4 eggs, separated
315 g (10 oz) sugar
500 g (1 lb) curd cheese
5 ml (1 tsp) vanilla extract
250 ml (8 fl oz) single cream**

**TOPPING
400 g (13 oz) canned strawberries
(drained, syrup reserved)
25 ml (5 tsp) cornflour**

❶ Divide sponge cake horizontally into three layers. Place one in bottom of 20 cm (8 inch) loose-bottomed cake tin. Freeze remaining layers for later use.

❷ Sponge gelatine in the 100 ml (3½ fl oz) water and dissolve over hot water.

❸ Beat egg yolks and 250 g (8 oz) sugar together in top of double boiler. Beat until light and fluffy while bringing to the boil.

❹ Remove from heat; stir in gelatine.

❺ Add curd cheese and extract, and fold in beaten egg whites.

❻ Beat cream with remaining sugar and add to egg mixture, beating lightly until smooth.

❼ Pour mixture over cake layer and leave to set in refrigerator.

❽ Arrange fruit on top of cheesecake.

❾ For syrup: Boil syrup from fruit in a saucepan; dissolve cornflour in syrup. Bring to the boil and simmer while stirring constantly until thickened.

❿ Spoon syrup over fruit and leave to set in refrigerator.

TIP

Sponging: Sprinkle powdered gelatine over cold water, leave for a few minutes to allow the gelatine to swell, then dissolve over boiling water.

RED VELVET CAKE

**125 g (4 oz) butter
250 g (8 oz) sugar
2 eggs
45 ml (3 tbsp) cocoa powder
30 ml (2 tbsp) red food colouring
280 g (9 oz) plain flour
2.5 ml (½ tsp) salt
250 ml (8 fl oz) buttermilk
5 ml (1 tsp) bicarbonate of soda
15 ml (1 tbsp) vinegar
5 ml (1 tsp) vanilla extract**

**ICING
60 ml (4 tbsp) plain flour
250 ml (8 fl oz) milk
90 g (3 oz) butter
90 g (3 oz) icing sugar
5 ml (1 tsp) vanilla extract
60 g (2 oz) desiccated coconut
30 g (1 oz) walnuts, chopped**

❶ Beat butter and sugar together. Add eggs, one at a time, beating well until light and fluffy.

❷ Make a paste of cocoa and food colouring. Add to butter mixture and beat well.

❸ Sift flour and salt and add alternately with buttermilk to creamed mixture.

❹ Dissolve bicarbonate of soda in vinegar and add, with vanilla extract, to mixture.

❺ Spoon mixture into two greased 20 cm (8 inch) cake tins and bake in a preheated oven at 180 °C (350 °F/gas 4) for 25–30 minutes.

❻ Leave in tin for a few minutes before turning out on to a wire rack to cool.

❼ For icing: Beat flour and milk together and bring to boil, stirring constantly until thickened.

❽ Remove from heat and stir in remaining ingredients.

❾ Ice cake when completely cold.

TIP

Instead of icing the cake, make an attractive pattern by dusting it with icing sugar sprinkled over a wire rack or patterned doily.

FRIENDSHIP CAKE

**280 g (9 oz) plain flour
10 g (⅓ oz) instant dry yeast
500 ml (16 fl oz) lukewarm water**

Combine all ingredients and leave to stand, covered, for 7 days, stirring once a day. Use a quarter of this mixture to start your cake.

Day 1: Add 250 g (8 oz) sugar, 150 g (5 oz) plain flour, 250 ml (8 fl oz) milk. Leave to rise.

Days 2, 3 and 4: Stir well. Cover and leave to rise.

Day 5: Again add 250 g (8 oz) sugar, 150 g (5 oz) plain flour, 250 ml (8 fl oz) milk.

Days 6, 7, 8 and 9: Stir well. Cover and leave to rise.

Day 10: Stir. Give a quarter of mixture and the recipe to each of three friends, keeping remainder. Make a delicious cake by adding to your mixture:

**250 ml (8 fl oz) cooking oil
3 eggs, beaten
250 g (8 oz) sugar
280 g (9 oz) plain flour
10 ml (2 tsp) baking powder
5 ml (1 tsp) bicarbonate of soda
10 ml (2 tsp) vanilla extract
5 ml (1 tsp) ground cinnamon
2.5 ml (½ tsp) ground ginger
2.5 ml (½ tsp) mixed spice
2.5 ml (½ tsp) ground cloves
375 g (12 oz) apple pie filling
150 g (5 oz) mixed dried fruit
60 g (2 oz) walnuts, chopped
optional
90 g (3 oz) desiccated coconut,
optional
icing sugar for dusting**

❶ Stir all ingredients together well, and spoon into a greased 23 cm (9 inch) ring tin or two greased 23 cm (9 inch) loaf tins and bake in a preheated oven at 160 °C (325 °F/gas 3) for 45 minutes (ring tin) or 50–60 minutes (loaf tin).

❷ Dust with icing sugar and serve hot or cold with cream.

TIP

If mixture more than doubles in size during standing, just stir again.

Clockwise from top: Red Velvet Cake, Friendship Cake and Low-Fat Cheesecake.

VENETIAN CAKE

60 g (2 oz) butter
60 ml (4 tbsp) sugar
2 large eggs
280 g (9 oz) plain flour
2.5 ml (½ tsp) salt
10 ml (2 tsp) baking powder
10 ml (2 tsp) vanilla extract

FILLING
625 ml (1 pint) milk
60(4 tbsp) ml sugar
2 egg yolks
15 ml (1 tbsp) plain flour
20 ml (4 tsp) custard powder
5 ml (1 tsp) vanilla extract

❶ In a saucepan, melt butter and beat in sugar. Add eggs, beating well after each addition.

❷ Sift dry ingredients together and add, with extract, to egg mixture.

❸ Mix to a stiff dough. Cover with cling film and rest for about 1 hour.

❹ Divide dough into six equal portions. Roll out each portion to cover base of an inverted, greased, round cake tin. Trim, reserving excess dough.

❺ Bake each layer for 4–5 minutes in a preheated oven at 200 °C (400 °F/ gas 6) until light brown.

❻ For filling: Bring milk and sugar to the boil.

❼ Beat egg yolks, flour and custard powder together with a little extra milk to make a smooth paste.

❽ Pour a little of the boiled sugar mixture into egg yolk mixture and then pour this mixture back into the rest of heated mixture. Return to hob and cook until thick, boiling for about 5 minutes. Add extract.

❾ Use filling to sandwich the six biscuit layers together, spreading the remaining filling on top. Sprinkle with extra dough, baked and crushed.

VARIATION

As an alternative filling, use any instant pudding such as vanilla or butterscotch.

BLACK FOREST GATEAU

CHOCOLATE CAKE
3 eggs
250 g (8 oz) caster sugar
45 ml (3 tbsp) water
60 ml (4 tbsp) milk
60 g (2 oz) butter or margarine
45 ml (3 tbsp) cocoa powder
210 g (7 oz) plain flour
10 ml (2 tsp) baking powder
2.5 ml (H tsp) salt
5 ml (1 tsp) vanilla extract

❶ For cake: Whisk eggs and sugar together until light and fluffy.

❷ Bring water, milk and butter to boil. Mix in cocoa powder.

❸ Sift flour, baking powder and salt together. Add to egg and sugar mixture gradually, beating continuously.

❹ Add boiled mixture and extract.

❺ Pour into two greased and lined 20 cm (8 inch) round cake tins and bake in a preheated oven at 180 °C (350 °F/gas 4) for 25–30 minutes.

❻ Leave in tins for a few minutes before turning on to a wire rack to cool. Cut each layer horizontally into two.

FILLING AND TOPPING
10 ml (2 tsp) sherry or kirsch liqueur
420 g (13½ oz) can black cherries, without stones, in syrup
750 ml (1¼ pints) whipping cream
200 g (6½ oz) plain chocolate, grated

❶ To assemble: Mix sherry with 125 ml (4 fl oz) cherry syrup.

❷ Place one layer of cake on a serving platter. Sprinkle with some of the cherry syrup.

❸ Cover with a thin layer of cream.

❹ Halve three-quarters of the cherries. Place a third of the halved cherries on the layer of cream.

❺ Place a second layer of cake over this and repeat until final cake layer has been used. Press layers down gently.

❻ Cover sides of cake with cream and sprinkle chocolate around sides.

❼ Spread a layer of cream over top and pipe rosettes of cream around edge.

❽ Place a drained whole cherry on each rosette and sprinkle chocolate curls in the centre of the cake.

TIP

To coat the sides of cake: Place decoration such as chopped nuts, chocolate vermicelli or grated chocolate on a sheet of greaseproof paper. Holding the cake at top and bottom, roll in the decoration until the sides are evenly coated.

EGGLESS CAKE

280 g (9 oz) self-raising flour
10 ml (2 tsp) baking powder
2.5 ml (½ tsp) bicarbonate of soda
125 g (4 oz) butter, melted
400 g (13 oz) condensed milk
about 150 ml (¼ pint) water
5 ml (1 tsp) vanilla extract

❶ Sift flour, baking powder and bicarbonate of soda together.

❷ Cool butter slightly and add, with condensed milk, water and extract, to dry ingredients.

❸ Beat until smooth and spoon into two greased and lined 20 cm (8 inch) cake tins.

❹ Bake in a preheated oven at 180 °C (350 °F/gas 4) for 20 minutes. Leave in tins for a few minutes before turning on to a wire rack to cool. Ice with Passion Fruit (page 66) or Lemon Icing (page 66).

TIP

This cake is suitable for cutting into shapes, and can be used as a base for fancy birthday cakes.

From top: Venetian Cake and Black Forest Gâteau.

CINNAMON CAKE

3 eggs, separated
250 g (8 oz) sugar
125 ml (4 fl oz) oil
125 ml (4 fl oz) water
150 g (5 oz) plain flour
30 ml (2 tbsp) cornflour
15 ml (3 tsp) baking powder
2.5 ml (½ tsp) salt
30 ml (2 tbsp) ground cinnamon

SYRUP
30 g (1 oz) butter
45 ml (3 tbsp) smooth apricot or plum jam
cinnamon sugar

❶ Whisk egg yolks, sugar, oil and water together.

❷ Sift dry ingredients together and add to above mixture.

❸ Beat egg whites until stiff and fold into mixture.

❹ Pour into a greased ovenproof dish about 18 x 28 cm (7 x 11 inches).

❺ Bake in a preheated oven at 190 ˚C (375 ˚F/gas 5) for 20–30 minutes.

❻ For syrup: Melt butter and jam.

❼ Take cake out of oven and prick well. Pour hot syrup over hot cake.

❽ Sprinkle with cinnamon sugar and serve hot.

TIPS

To make cinnamon sugar, mix 90 g (3 oz) sugar with 10 ml (2 tsp) ground cinnamon.

Cinnamon is usually bought ready-ground for use in sweet and savoury dishes and in cakes.

SWISS ROLL

4 eggs, separated
165 g (5½ oz) caster sugar
45 ml (3 tbsp) cold water
110 g (3½ oz) self-raising flour
2.5 ml (½ tsp) salt
smooth jam, any flavour
icing sugar

❶ Whisk egg yolks. Gradually add sugar, whisking all the time, until thick. Whisk in cold water.

❷ Beat egg whites until stiff but not dry, and add, with the sifted dry ingredients, to egg yolk mixture. Fold in gently with a metal spoon.

❸ Line a 23 x 32 cm (9 x 13 inch) Swiss roll tin with greaseproof paper. Grease well and turn mixture into tin. Bake in a preheated oven at 180 ˚C (350 ˚F/gas 4) for 20 minutes.

❹ Turn out immediately onto a cloth well sprinkled with caster sugar. Peel off paper lining and trim edges of cake using a sharp knife. Roll up cake with cloth to make Swiss roll. Cover with a damp cloth and allow to cool slightly.

❺ Place jam in a double boiler over hot water until warm. Unroll cake and spread with jam. Roll up with the aid of a cloth and allow to cool. Dust lightly with icing sugar before serving.

VARIATIONS

Fill with strawberry or apricot jam and cream beaten with 60 ml (4 tbsp) grated or chopped chocolate.

CHOCOLATE SWISS ROLL

Add 25 ml (5 tsp) cocoa powder and 2.5 ml (½ tsp) instant coffee powder to the dry ingredients. Fill with whipped cream and sprinkle with a grated peppermint crisp or chopped chocolate. Roll up.

HAZELNUT SWISS ROLL

Add 75 g (2½ oz) chopped or ground toasted hazelnuts to the dry ingredients.

TIPS

The cake will roll best while still warm, so speed is essential for producing an unbroken and evenly rolled cake.

Make sure that the cake is completely cold before spreading with the filling.

GREEK SEMOLINA CAKE

340 g (11 oz) butter
250 g (8 oz) sugar
6 eggs, separated
10 ml (2 tsp) grated orange rind
280 g (9 oz) plain flour
165 g (5½ oz) semolina
20 ml (4 tsp) baking powder
2.5 ml (½ tsp) salt
250 ml (8 fl oz) orange juice
75 ml (5 tbsp) flaked almonds

SYRUP
500 g (1 lb) sugar
500 ml (16 fl oz) water
30 ml (2 tbsp) brandy (optional)

❶ Beat butter and 125 g (4 oz) of the sugar together. Add egg yolks and beat well after each addition until light and fluffy. Add orange rind.

❷ Beat egg whites until foamy. Add remaining sugar gradually, beating until egg whites are stiff, but not dry.

❸ Sift dry ingredients together and stir, with orange juice, into the creamed mixture. Fold in meringue.

❹ Turn into a greased 22 x 32 cm (9 x 13 inch) rectangular dish. Sprinkle with almonds.

❺ Bake in a preheated oven at 180 ˚C (350 ˚F/gas 4) for 40–45 minutes. Allow to cool slightly.

❻ For syrup: Dissolve sugar in water and bring to the boil. Simmer for 5 minutes, add brandy, and pour over lukewarm cake.

❼ Cool and cut into squares.

VARIATION

Substitute Grand Marnier or Cointreau for brandy.

56

Clockwise from top: Hot Milk Sponge, Swiss Roll, Cinnamon Cake and Greek Semolina Cake.

HOT MILK SPONGE

4 eggs
315 g (10 oz) caster sugar
280 g (9 oz) plain flour
15 ml (1 tbsp) baking powder
250 ml (8 fl oz) milk
90 g (3 oz) butter or margarine
5 ml (1 tsp) vanilla extract

❶ Beat eggs and sugar together until thick and light yellow.

❷ Sift flour and baking powder to-gether and fold into egg and sugar mixture.

❸ Heat milk and butter. Do not boil.

❹ Stir milk mixture and extract into batter. Spoon into two greased 20 cm (8 inch) cake tins.

❺ Bake in a preheated oven at 180 °C (350 °F/gas 4) for 25–30 minutes.

TIP

Use hot milk sponge for birthday cakes for the children, for baked Alaska or for trifle.

Make sure that the cake has cooled completely before you begin icing.

APPLE CAKE

2 eggs
250 g (8 oz) sugar
60 ml (4 tbsp) milk
30 g (1 oz) margarine, melted
150 g (5 oz) self-raising flour
375 g (12 oz) can apple pie filling

SAUCE
250 g (8 oz) sugar
125 ml (4 fl oz) single cream
5 ml (1 tsp) caramel extract

❶ Whisk eggs and sugar. Add milk and melted margarine.

❷ Add flour, mix until smooth, and pour batter into a greased dish about 18 x 28 cm (7 x 11 inches), or a round 23 cm (9 inch) pie dish.

❸ Arrange apples on batter and bake in a preheated oven at 180 ˚C (350 ˚F/gas 4) for 25–30 minutes.

❹ For sauce: Combine sugar and cream, bring to the boil, and add extract. Pour over hot cake after removing from oven.

ORANGE BUTTER CAKE

250 g (8 oz) butter or margarine
315 g (10 oz) caster sugar
4 eggs
20 ml (4 tps) grated orange rind
5 ml (1 tsp) vanilla extract
280 g (9 oz) self-raising flour
2.5 ml (½ tsp) salt
about 150 ml (¼ pint) milk

❶ Cream butter and sugar together well. Add eggs, one at a time, and beat well after each addition until light and fluffy. Add orange rind and extract.

❷ Sift flour and salt together and add, together with milk, to egg mixture.

❸ Spoon the mixture into a greased and lined 20 x 25 cm (8 x 10 inch) rectangular tin.

❹ Bake in a preheated oven at 180 ˚C (350 ˚F/gas 4) for 40–45 minutes.

❺ Leave in tin a while, then turn on to a wire rack to cool. Ice with Orange Icing (page 66). Cut into squares.

PETITS FOURS

GENOISE SPONGE
4 eggs
125 g (4 oz) caster sugar
150 g (5 oz) plain flour
2.5 ml (½ tsp) salt
60 g (2 oz) butter, melted and cooled

FILLING
165 g (5½ oz) sieved apricot jam
20 ml (4 tsp) water

TOPPING
250 g (8 oz) marzipan (almond paste)
icing sugar

GLACE ICING
560 g (1 lb 2 oz) icing sugar
15 ml (1 tbsp) butter
about 30 ml (2 tbsp) boiling water
few drops vanilla, almond or orange extract or coffee powder
colouring of choice

❶ For sponge: Whisk eggs and sugar together until pale and thick.

❷ Sift flour and salt together; fold into mixture alternately with melted butter.

❸ Pour into a lined and greased 23 x 32 cm (9 x 13 inch) rectangular tin. Bake in a preheated oven at 180 ˚C (350 ˚F/gas 4) for 15–20 minutes, until lightly browned and firm.

❹ Turn out on to wire rack, remove lining paper and cool completely. Divide cake into two horizontally.

❺ For filling: Heat apricot jam and water and brush half over one layer, covering with second layer. Press down well and brush the top of cake with remaining jam.

❻ For topping: Knead marzipan until smooth. Dust with icing sugar and roll out thinly into a rectangle. Cover sponge with marzipan. Place greaseproof paper over and leave for 24 hours. Remove paper and use cutters to cut into various shapes, such as triangles, ovals, squares and diamonds.

❼ For glacé icing: Mix all ingredients together to form a smooth and pouring consistency. Pour over petits fours to coat and leave to set. Decorate with chocolate, glacé cherries and angelica.

Makes 40

VARIATIONS

Replace apricot jam with Chocolate Cream, and Glacé Icing with Chocolate Glacé Icing

CHOCOLATE CREAM

90 g (3 oz) butter
15 ml (1 tbsp) cocoa powder
2.5 ml (½ tsp) coffee powder
20 ml (4 tsp) boiling water
2.5 ml (½ tsp) vanilla extract
180 g (6 oz) icing sugar
Beat all ingredients until light and thick.

CHOCOLATE GLACE ICING

Add 25 ml (5 tsp) cocoa powder to icing sugar when making glacé icing.

CHOCOLATE BROWNIES

125 g (4 oz) plain cooking chocolate
125 g (4 oz) butter
15 ml (1 tbsp) golden syrup
3 eggs
500 g (1 lb) sugar
210 g (7 oz) plain flour
pinch salt
5 ml (1 tsp) vanilla extract
60 g (2 oz) pecan nuts, chopped

❶ Melt chocolate, butter and syrup together and mix until smooth.

❷ Beat eggs and sugar together until light and fluffy.

❸ Sift dry ingredients together and add, with melted chocolate mixture, to creamed egg mixture.

❹ Add extract and nuts.

❺ Pour mixture into a greased 20 x 25 cm (8 x 10 inch) rectangular tin and bake in a preheated oven at 160 ˚C (325 ˚F/gas 3) for 40–45 minutes. Cool completely in tin, then cut into squares.

Makes 20

Cakes

Clockwise from top: Petits Fours, Orange Butter Cake and Apple Cake.

59

LAMINGTONS

250 g (8 oz) butter or margarine
500 g (1 lb) sugar
4 eggs
125 ml (4 fl oz) milk
470 g (15 oz) plain flour
10 ml (2 tsp) baking powder
2.5 ml (½ tsp) salt

CHOCOLATE SYRUP
600 g (1¼ lb) sugar
75 g (2½ oz) cocoa powder
375 ml (¾ pint) water
15 ml (1 tbsp) butter or margarine
desiccated coconut

❶ Beat butter and sugar together. Add eggs, and beat well after each addition until light and fluffy.

❷ Add milk and mix well.

❸ Sift flour, baking powder and salt together, and add to egg mixture.

❹ Spoon dough into a greased baking tin about 25 x 30 cm (10 x 12 inches) or into two 23 cm (9 inch) square cake tins. Bake in a preheated oven at 180 °C (350 °F/gas 4) for 50–60 minutes. Cut into squares and leave to cool.

❺ For syrup: Mix sugar, cocoa and water and bring to boil while stirring constantly. Add butter or margarine. While still warm, dip the cake squares in syrup, but do not soak. Roll squares in a thick layer of coconut spread on a large sheet of greaseproof paper.

❻ Place on a wire rack to set.

Makes 42

VARIATIONS

WHITE SYRUP

600 g (1¼ lb) sugar
250 ml (8 fl oz) water
3 egg whites

Bring sugar and water to boil, and boil for 5 minutes. Beat egg whites until stiff. Gradually pour syrup on to egg whites and leave to cool.

COLOURED LAMINGTONS

For coloured Lamingtons, colour coconut with food colourings.

TIPS

One-day-old cake is ideal for making Lamingtons as it cuts more easily when a little stale. Alternatively, place in the deep-freeze for a while for easier cutting. Sponge can be frozen for 3–6 months.

Spear each piece of cake with a fork and dip into syrup. Hold over bowl for a moment to allow syrup to set slightly.

BANANA AND WALNUT BREAD

60 g (2 oz) butter
125 g (4 oz) caster sugar
1 egg, beaten
3 large bananas, mashed
280 g (9 oz) self-raising flour
2.5 ml (½ tsp) salt
75 ml (5 tbsp) milk
75 ml (5 tbsp) coarsely chopped walnuts, optional
5 ml (1 tsp) vanilla extract

❶ Beat butter and sugar together until the mixture is light and creamy.

❷ Add egg and mashed bananas, beating thoroughly.

❸ Sift flour and salt together and add alternately with milk to creamed mixture. Add walnuts and extract.

❹ Pour into a greased 23 cm (9 inch) loaf tin and bake in a preheated oven at 180 °C (350 °F/gas 4) for 1 hour.

❺ Leave in tin for a few minutes before turning on to a wire rack to cool. Serve with butter.

TIP

To prevent the bowl from slipping while mixing, and to reduce noise, place a damp cloth underneath your mixing bowl.

CHOCOLATE PUMPKIN LOAF

125 g (4 oz) butter
10 ml (2 tsp) grated orange rind
125 g (4 oz) caster sugar
1 egg
15 ml (1 tbsp) golden syrup
210 g (7 oz) well-drained cold, mashed pumpkin
165 g (5½ oz) self-raising flour
2.5 ml (½ tsp) bicarbonate of soda
30 ml (2 tbsp) cocoa powder
15 ml (1 tbsp) custard powder
60 ml (4 tbsp) orange juice

ICING
180 g (6 oz) icing sugar
15 ml (1 tbsp) cocoa powder
5 ml (1 tsp) butter
15 ml (1 tbsp) milk

❶ Beat butter, rind and sugar together. Add egg and syrup and beat well.

❷ Stir in pumpkin and dry ingredients alternately with orange juice.

❸ Pour mixture into a lined and greased 23 cm (9 inch) loaf tin and bake in a preheated oven at 180 °C (350 °F/gas 4) for 1 hour. Leave loaf in the tin for a few minutes before turning on to a wire rack to cool.

❹ For icing: Sift icing sugar, add remaining ingredients, and beat until smooth. Spread icing over cooled loaf.

TIP

Cake can be stored in the refrigerator for a few days.

Clockwise from top: Lamingtons, Chocolate Pumpkin Loaf and Banana and Walnut Bread.

YOGHURT LOAF

125 g (4 oz) butter
15 ml (1 tbsp) grated orange rind
250 g (8 oz) caster sugar
3 eggs, separated
90 g (3 oz) mixed peel, chopped
60 ml (4 tbsp) orange juice
280 g (9 oz) self-raising flour
250 ml (8 fl oz) low-fat plain yoghurt

ORANGE ICING
280 g (9 oz) icing sugar
30 g (1 oz) butter, softened
5 ml (1 tsp) grated orange rind
30 ml (1 tbsp) orange juice

❶ Beat butter, rind and sugar together in a bowl until light and creamy. Beat in egg yolks one at a time. Stir in mixed peel and orange juice.

❷ Sift flour and add to mixture alternately with yoghurt.

❸ Beat egg whites to soft peak stage and fold lightly into mixture.

❹ Pour into a lined and greased 23 cm (9 inch) loaf tin and bake in a preheated oven at 150 °C (300 °F/ gas 2) for 1¼ hours. Leave in tin for a few minutes; cool on a wire rack.

❺ For icing: Combine icing sugar, butter and rind. Stir in enough juice to mix icing to a spreading consistency. Ice cake.

TIP

The texture of this cake is very soft, so it is best not to remove the lining paper until the cake has cooled.

GINGERBREAD

280 g (9 oz) plain flour
5 ml (1 tsp) baking powder
10 ml (2 tsp) ground ginger
2.5 ml (½ tsp) mixed spice
2.5 ml (½ tsp) salt
2.5 ml (½ tsp) bicarbonate of soda
90 g (3 oz) soft brown sugar
250 g (8 oz) golden syrup
60 g (2 oz) margarine
2 eggs
200 ml (6½ fl oz) milk
45 g (1½ oz) crystallized ginger, chopped

❶ Sift dry ingredients together and add brown sugar.

❷ Melt syrup and margarine together, but do not boil.

❸ Whisk eggs and milk together.

❹ Gradually stir syrup mixture into egg mixture.

❺ Make a well in the centre of the dry ingredients; stir in liquid and crystallized ginger. Beat the mixture well until smooth.

❻ Pour into a well-greased 23 cm (9 inch) loaf tin. Bake gingerbread in a preheated oven at 160 °C (325 °F/gas 3) for 1¼ hours.

VARIATION

MUFFINS

Add 90 g (3 oz) sultanas to ingredients. Spoon into well-greased muffin tins and bake at 180 °C (350 °F/gas 4) for 20 minutes.

CHERRY LOAF

200 g (6½ oz) butter, softened
1 egg, beaten
5 ml (1 tsp) vanilla extract
340 mg (11 oz) plain flour
10 ml (2 tsp) baking powder
2.5 ml (½ tsp) salt
110 g (3½ oz) red glacé cherries, halved
125 ml (4 fl oz) water
210 g (7 oz) can condensed milk

❶ Cream butter, and add egg and extract. Sift dry ingredients together and add cherries. Add, with remaining ingredients, to creamed mixture.

❷ Spoon into a lined and greased 23 cm (9 inch) loaf tin.

❸ Bake in a preheated oven at 190 °C (375 °F/gas 5) for 50–60 minutes.

❹ Turn on to a wire rack to cool.

TIPS

This cake can be successfully made in a food processor.

Roll cherries in flour to prevent them from sinking to the bottom.

DATE LOAF

250 g (8 oz) stoned dates, chopped
5 ml (1 tsp) bicarbonate of soda
250 ml (8 fl oz) boiling water
30 ml (2 tbsp) margarine
200 g (6½ oz) sugar
1 egg
280 g (9 oz) plain flour
5 ml (1 tsp) baking powder
1.25 ml (¼ tsp) salt
5 ml (1 tsp) vanilla extract

❶ Place dates in a bowl. Dissolve bicarbonate of soda in boiling water and pour over dates.

❷ Beat margarine and sugar together. Add egg, beating until light and fluffy.

❸ Sift dry ingredients and add alternately with dates and water to egg mixture. Add extract.

❹ Spoon mixture into a lined and greased 23 cm (9 inch) loaf tin and bake in a preheated oven at 160 °C (325 °F/gas 3) for 50–55 minutes.

❺ Leave loaf in tin for a few minutes before turning out on to a wire rack to cool.

TIP

Dates can be bought whole, as plump and shiny table dates to be eaten as they are, or pressed into slabs suitable for cooking.

Clockwise from top left: Cherry Loaf, Date Loaf, Nutty Almond Cake and Yoghurt Loaf.

NUTTY ALMOND CAKE

200 g (6½ oz) sugar
125 ml (4 fl oz) cooking oil
125 ml (4 fl oz) milk
340 g (11 oz) self-raising flour
pinch salt
200 g (6½ oz) curd cheese

TOPPING
150 g (5 oz) butter, melted
200 g (6½ oz) sugar
60 ml (4 tbsp) desiccated coconut
110 g (3½ oz) flaked almond
110 g (3½ oz) chopped mixed nuts

❶ Whisk sugar, oil and milk together.

❷ Sift flour and salt together and add to sugar mixture.

❸ Add curd cheese and mix well.

❹ Spread on the base of a greased 23 x 32 cm (9 x 13 inch) rectangular dish or cake tin.

❺ For topping: Mix all ingredients together; spread over cake mixture.

❻ Bake in a preheated oven at 200 °C (400 °F/gas 6) for 10 minutes; then reduce heat to 180 °C (350 °F/gas 4) and bake for a further 20 minutes.

❼ Cool and cut into squares or slices.

<u>VARIATION</u>

Substitute coconut for nuts if preferred.

63

MADEIRA CAKE

125 g (4 oz) butter
250 g (8 oz) caster sugar
2 eggs
10 ml (2 tsp) grated lemon rind
5 ml (1 tsp) vanilla extract
280 g (9 oz) plain flour
10 ml (2 tsp) baking powder
250 ml (8 fl oz) milk

❶ Beat butter and sugar together well.

❷ Beat in eggs, lemon rind and extract until mixture is light and fluffy.

❸ Sift the flour and baking powder together and mix into the creamed mixture alternately with milk.

❹ Pour the mixture into a well-greased 23 cm (9 inch) loaf tin and bake in a preheated oven at 180 °C (350 °F/gas 4) for 1 hour.

VARIATION

CARAWAY SEED CAKE

Add 10 ml (2 tsp) caraway seeds to creamed mixture.

TIP

To soften butter in the microwave: Place in a small microwave bowl and cover with paper towel. Cook on High or 100% power until soft but not melted. 125 g (4 oz) butter takes about 45 seconds.

EASY FRUIT LOAF

180 g (6 oz) soft brown sugar
250 ml (8 fl oz) milk
250 g (8 oz) butter or margarine
250 g (8 oz) mixed dried fruit
60 g (2 oz) glacé cherries, chopped
1 egg, beaten
340 g (11 oz) plain flour
5 ml (1 tsp) baking powder
2.5 ml (½ tsp) bicarbonate of soda
5 ml (1 tsp) mixed spice

❶ Place sugar, milk, butter, dried fruit and cherries in a saucepan. Bring to boil, then simmer for 2–3 minutes. Allow to cool.

❷ Add beaten egg to mixture. Sift dry ingredients together, add to mixture, and mix well.

❸ Pour into a greased and well-lined 23 cm (9 inch) loaf tin.

❹ Bake in a preheated oven at 160 °C (325 °F/gas 3) for 1¼ hours. Leave for a few minutes in tin before turning on to a wire rack to cool.

TIP

Test whether the cake is cooked by inserting a skewer into the centre. If it is baked, the skewer will come out clean.

VARIATIONS

Pour this syrup over hot loaf:
125 ml (4 fl oz) fresh orange juice
10 ml (2 tsp) fresh lemon juice
2.5 ml (½ tsp) grated orange rind
125 g (4 oz) caster sugar
Boil ingredients together for 5 minutes, then leave to cool slightly before pouring over cake.

Add 60 g (2 oz) chopped pecan nuts or walnuts, chopped, to mixture.

COURGETTE LOAF

250 ml (8 fl oz) cooking oil
250 g (8 oz) sugar
3 eggs
150 g (5 oz) plain flour
150 g (5 oz) granary flour
5 ml (1 tsp) baking powder
2.5 ml (½ tsp) bicarbonate of soda
2.5 ml (½ tsp) salt
pinch grated nutmeg
15 ml (1 tbsp) ground cinnamon
250 g (8 oz) courgettes, finely grated
90 g (3 oz) seedless raisins
5 ml (1 tsp) vanilla extract

❶ Whisk oil and sugar together. Add eggs, beating well after each addition.

❷ Sift dry ingredients together, add bran left behind in sieve. Add dry ingredients alternately with courgette, to creamed mixture.

❸ Stir in raisins and extract, and spoon into a lined 23 cm (9 inch) loaf tin. Bake in a preheated oven at 160 °C (325 °F/gas 3) for 50–60 minutes.

TIPS

Large courgettes are delicious hollowed out and stuffed with a savoury filling such as onion, cheese, bacon and parsley, and then grilled or baked.

It is not necessary to peel courgettes before cooking.

Clockwise from top: Courgette Loaf, Easy Fruit Loaf and Madeira Cake.

CAKE ICING

Icing is more than just a decoration on cakes. It prevents drying out and adds flavour to bland cakes or biscuits.

Colour and flavour the icing according to your personal taste.

Hints for icing cakes

● Allow cake to cool completely before icing and decorating. If cake is still slightly warm, icing will melt and run off surface.

● Brush all loose crumbs off surface of cake before icing.

● The icing surface should be flat. Turn cake over and use base or, alternatively, trim top of cake to level it.

● Delicate cakes should be iced with a soft icing mix to prevent the cake from crumbling.

● When coating a cake with soft icing, do so on a wire rack. Spread icing while soft, using a palette knife.

● If a filling and an icing are used, place filling between layers before icing the cake or biscuit.

● When icing a cake with butter icing, cover the sides of the cake before icing the top.

● If the sides of the cake are to be covered with nuts, praline or chocolate vermicelli, first sandwich the layers together, then cover the sides with icing. Turn the cake on to its side, and gently roll the edges in the coating of your choice.

● Do not overmix the icing as this will result in a runny mixture.

BASIC ICING

110 g (3½ oz) butter, softened
375 g (12 oz) icing sugar
10 ml (2 tsp) vanilla extract
about 25 ml (5 tsp) milk

❶ Cream butter, icing sugar and extract. Add enough milk to make mixture light and creamy, with a spreadable consistency.

❷ Sandwich the layers together with icing, then ice the top of the cake.

CHOCOLATE BUTTER ICING

100 g (3½ oz) soft butter
375 g (12 oz) icing sugar
30 ml (2 tbsp) cocoa powder
30 ml (2 tbsp) hot water
5 ml (1 tsp) vanilla extract
about 25 ml (5 tsp) milk

❶ Cream butter and icing sugar, beating well until smooth. Dissolve cocoa powder in hot water and add to icing.

❷ Add extract and enough milk to make mixture light and creamy, with a spreadable consistency.

❸ Sandwich layers together with icing and ice the top of the cake.

MOCHA ICING

100 g (3½ oz) butter, softened
375 g (12 oz) icing sugar
30 ml (2 tbsp) cocoa powder
10 ml (2 tsp) strong coffee powder
30 ml (2 tbsp) hot water
about 25 ml (5 tsp) milk

❶ Cream butter and icing sugar. Dissolve cocoa powder and coffee powder in hot water and add to icing.

❷ Add enough milk to make mixture light and creamy, with a spreadable consistency.

❸ Sandwich layers together with icing, then ice the top of the cake.

ORANGE ICING

60 g (2 oz) butter, softened
375 g (12 oz) icing sugar
5 ml (1 tsp) grated orange rind
45 ml (3 tbsp) orange juice

❶ Cream butter, icing sugar and rind together. Add enough juice to make mixture light and creamy, with a spreadable consistency.

❷ Sandwich layers together with icing, then ice the top of the cake.

LEMON ICING

30 ml (2 tbsp) butter, softened
280 g (9 oz) icing sugar
5 ml (1 tsp) grated lemon rind
15 ml (1 tbsp) lemon juice

❶ Cream butter, icing sugar and rind together. Add enough juice to make mixture light and creamy, with a spreadable consistency.

❷ Sandwich layers together with icing, then ice the top of the cake.

PASSION FRUIT ICING

30 ml (2 tbsp) butter, softened
470 g (15 oz) icing sugar
110 g (3½ oz) can passion fruit pulp

❶ Cream butter, icing sugar and passion fruit pulp together until light and creamy, with a spreadable consistency.

❷ Sandwich layers together with icing, then ice the top of the cake.

CARAMEL ICING

60 g (2 oz) butter, softened
45 ml (3 tbsp) soft brown sugar
280 g (9 oz) icing sugar
5 ml (1 tsp) caramel extract
about 25 ml (5 tsp) milk

❶ Cream butter and sugar together. Add icing sugar, extract and enough milk to make icing light and creamy.

❷ Sandwich layers together with icing and ice the top of the cake.

Clockwise from top left: Chocolate Butter Icing, Lemon Icing, Passion Fruit Icing, Royal Icing, Glacé Icing and Mocha Icing.

CREAM CHEESE ICING

100 g (3½ oz) butter, softened
375 g (12 oz) icing sugar
125 g (4 oz) cream or curd cheese
5 ml (1 tsp) vanilla extract

❶ Cream butter, icing sugar, cream or curd cheese and extract together until mixture is light and creamy and has a spreadable consistency.

❷ Sandwich layers together with icing, then ice top of cake.

GLACE ICING

Use this icing while still warm. First glaze cake with apricot jam so that no crumbs mix with the icing.

180 g (6 oz) icing sugar
about 30 ml (2 tbsp) boiling water
2.5 ml (½ tsp) vanilla extract or lemon juice
few drops of food colouring

❶ Sift icing sugar and add enough water to make a smooth consistency.

❷ Add extract and colouring. Dip a skewer into the bottle and add to icing to avoid using too much colouring.

ROYAL ICING

This quick-and-easy fruit cake icing is traditionally used on top of a layer of marzipan and will protect the cake for months.

1 egg white
560 g (1 lb 2 oz) icing sugar
5 ml (1 tsp) lemon juice

❶ Beat egg white until foamy. Gradually beat in icing sugar, beating well after each addition.

❷ When mixture reaches soft peak stage, beat in lemon juice. Continue to add icing sugar and beat until stiff.

6

MUFFINS

MUFFINS ARE QUICK AND EASY TO MAKE USING SWEET OR SAVOURY INGREDIENTS AND CAN BE SERVED ON ANY DAY OF THE YEAR! ADD LOTS OF BRAN TO MAKE THEM NUTRITIOUS.
THESE MUFFINS ARE USUALLY REFERRED TO AS AMERICAN MUFFINS TO DISTINGUISH THEM FROM ENGLISH MUFFINS, WHICH ARE ROUND YEAST CAKES SIMILAR TO CRUMPETS.

GUIDELINES FOR MAKING MUFFINS

● Handle batter lightly. Mix liquids into the dry ingredients, stirring just enough to moisten. The batter should still look lumpy.

● Overmixing the batter will destroy the light texture of the muffins and can result in tough, coarse muffins that contain tunnels.

● Fill the muffin tins two-thirds full, spooning in the batter in one scoop. If muffin tins are not available, spoon batter into paper cake cases placed on a baking tray.

● To test whether they are done, press down gently on top of muffin. If it springs back, the muffins are ready.

● Muffins are best when freshly baked. They are delicious served warm and buttered.

Freezing muffins

Muffins can be successfully frozen for up to 3 months. Cool slightly, then, while still warm, freeze in foil or an airtight container to preserve moisture. Reheat frozen in foil in an oven at 200 °C (400 °F/gas 6) for 12–15 minutes. Or microwave frozen muffin in paper towel on High/100% power for 30–45 seconds.

30-DAY HEALTH MUFFINS

The mixture for these delicious, healthy muffins can be stored in an airtight container in the refrigerator for up to 30 days, and used as needed.

2 eggs
125 ml (4 fl oz) cooking oil
280 g (9 oz) soft brown sugar
500 ml (16 fl oz) milk
150 g (5 oz) granary flour
210 g (7 oz) plain flour
60 g (2 oz) bran OR
150 g (5 oz) granary flour
5 ml (1 tsp) salt
5 ml (1 tsp) vanilla extract
10 ml (2 tsp) bicarbonate of soda
150 g (5 oz) mixed dried fruit
150 g (5 oz) stoned dates, chopped

❶ Whisk eggs, oil and sugar together.

❷ Add remaining ingredients and mix until combined.

❸ Pour the mixture into an airtight container and allow to stand in the refrigerator overnight.

❹ Spoon into well-greased muffin tins, filling each two-thirds full. Bake in a preheated oven at 180 °C (350 °F/gas 4) for 20–25 minutes.

❺ Serve hot with butter.

Makes 48

VARIATIONS

Add 125 g (4 oz) chopped walnuts or pecan nuts to the mixture.

Replace mixed dried fruit and dates with 315 g (10 oz) sultanas or raisins.

15 ml (1 tbsp) grated orange rind may also be added to ingredients.

BLUEBERRY MUFFINS

75 g (2½ oz) granary flour
210 g (7 oz) plain flour
15 ml (1 tbsp) baking powder
200 g (6½ oz) caster sugar
2.5 ml (½ tsp) salt
1 egg
125 ml (4 fl oz) milk
90 ml (6 tbsp) oil
440 g (14 oz) can blueberries, well drained

❶ Sift dry ingredients together and add bran left behind in sieve.

❷ Whisk egg, milk and oil together and mix into dry ingredients. Mix until flour is moistened; batter should still be lumpy. Add blueberries, being careful not to overmix.

❸ Spoon into greased muffin tins, filling each two-thirds full. Bake in a preheated oven at 200 °C (400 °F/gas 6) for 15–20 minutes, until golden brown. Serve hot with butter.

Makes 12

VARIATION

RASPBERRY MUFFINS

Replace blueberries with canned raspberries.

TIP

These muffins are not suitable for freezing.

From top: Blueberry Muffins and 30-day Health Muffins.

APPLE AND RAISIN MUFFINS

125 g (4 oz) margarine
125 g (4 oz) sugar
2 eggs
375 g (12 oz) canned apple pie filling, chopped
90 g (3 oz) raisins
250 ml (8 fl oz) milk
2.5 ml (½ tsp) vanilla extract
280 g (9 oz) plain flour
OR
150 g (5 oz) granary flour and
125 g (4 oz) plain flour
20 ml (4 tsp) baking powder
2.5 ml (½ tsp) salt
cinnamon sugar

❶ Beat margarine and sugar together. Add eggs and beat until mixture is light and fluffy.

❷ Stir in apples, raisins, milk and extract until thoroughly mixed. Add to sifted dry ingredients and mix until flour is moistened; batter should still be lumpy.

❸ Spoon into greased muffin tins, filling each about two-thirds full and sprinkle with cinnamon sugar. Bake in a preheated oven at 200 °C (400 °F/ gas 6) for 20–25 minutes.

❹ Serve hot with butter.

Makes 18

VARIATIONS

PINEAPPLE MUFFINS

Replace apples and raisins with 420 g (13½ oz) can crushed pineapple, with syrup.

CARROT MUFFINS

Replace apples with 180 g (6 oz) grated carrot, and add 2.5 ml (½ tsp) allspice and 5 ml (1 tsp) ground cinnamon to dry ingredients.

TIP

To soften hardened sugar, place a lemon in the sugar jar; after a few hours the sugar will have softened.

NUTTY WHEAT BANANA AND DATE MUFFINS

150 g (5 oz) granary flour
5 ml (1 tsp) baking powder
2.5 ml (½ tsp) ground cinnamon
75 g (2½ oz) wheatgerm
1 egg
75 ml (5 tbsp) cooking oil
90 g (3 oz) soft brown sugar
5 ml (1 tsp) bicarbonate of soda
45 ml (3 tbsp) milk
2 bananas, mashed
60 g (2 oz) stoned dates, chopped

❶ Sift granary flour, baking powder and ground cinnamon together. Add bran left in sieve and wheatgerm.

❷ Whisk egg, oil and sugar together, and mix into dry ingredients.

❸ Dissolve bicarbonate of soda in milk and stir, with bananas and dates, into dry ingredients. Mix until flour is moistened; batter should still be lumpy. Do not overmix.

❹ Spoon mixture into greased muffin tins, filling each two-thirds full.

❺ Bake in a preheated oven at 200 °C (400 °F/gas 6) for 20 minutes. Leave in tin a few minutes before turning on to a wire rack to cool.

❻ Serve hot with butter.

Makes 12

NUTTY WHEAT MARMALADE MUFFINS

210 g (7 oz) granary flour
150 g (5 oz) plain flour
20 ml (4 tsp) baking powder
2.5 ml (½ tsp) salt
75 ml (5 tbsp) oil
250 ml (8 fl oz) milk
2 eggs
90 g (3 oz) soft brown sugar
90 g (3 oz) mixed dried fruit
75 ml (5 tbsp) orange marmalade

❶ Sift dry ingredients together. Add bran left behind in sieve.

❷ Whisk oil, milk, eggs and sugar together. Add dried fruit and marmalade.

❸ Add liquid ingredients to dry ingredients; mix until flour is moistened. Batter should still be lumpy.

❹ Spoon mixture into muffin tins until half-full. Spoon 5 ml (1 tsp) marmalade on top and then cover with more mixture until muffin tins are two-thirds full.

❺ Bake in a preheated oven at 180 °C (350 °F/gas 4) for 15–20 minutes.

Makes 12

VARIATIONS

Any jam can be used instead of marmalade.

As an alternative, the marmalade or jam can be mixed into the batter.

Clockwise from top left: Nutty Wheat Marmalade Muffins, Apple and Raisin Muffins and Nutty Wheat Banana and Date Muffins.

DATE AND WALNUT MUFFINS

280 g (9 oz) plain flour
10 ml (2 tsp) baking powder
2.5 (½ tsp) ml salt
750 ml (5 tbsp) soft brown sugar
60 g (2 oz) margarine
125 g (4 oz) stoned dates, chopped
60 g (2 oz) walnuts or
pecan nuts, chopped
125 ml (4 fl oz) milk
1 egg

❶ Sift flour, baking powder and salt. Add sugar. Rub in margarine; add dates and nuts.

❷ Whisk milk and egg, and mix into dry ingredients. Mix until flour is moistened; batter should still be lumpy.

❸ Spoon mixture into greased muffin tins, filling each two-thirds full.

❹ Bake in a preheated oven at 190 °C (375 °F/gas 5) for 20 minutes.

❺ Serve hot with butter.

Makes 12

TIP

Chop dates using a knife that has been dipped in flour

LEMON MUFFINS

125 g (4 oz) margarine
125 g (4 oz) caster sugar
2 eggs
250 g (8 oz) plain flour
5 ml (1 tsp) baking powder
2.5 ml (½ tsp) bicarbonate of soda
pinch salt
10 ml (2 tsp) grated lemon rind
90 ml (6 tbsp) lemon juice

❶ Beat margarine and sugar together. Add eggs and beat until light and fluffy.

❷ Sift dry ingredients and add, with rind and juice, to creamed mixture until flour is moistened; batter should still be lumpy. Do not overmix.

---

❸ Spoon mixture into greased muffin tins, filling each two-thirds full. Bake in a preheated oven at 200 °C (400 °F/gas 6) for 20 minutes.

❹ Serve hot with butter.

Makes 12

TIP

A medium-sized lemon yields about 45 ml (3 tbsp) juice. To extract maximum juice, warm a whole lemon in a preheated moderate oven for 2 minutes.

SPINACH MUFFINS

210 g (7 oz) plain flour
10 ml (2 tsp) baking powder
2.5 ml (½ tsp) salt
pinch cayenne pepper
180 g (6 oz) cooked chopped spinach
125 g (4 oz) rindless streaky bacon, chopped
125 g (4 oz) Cheddar cheese, grated
90 ml (6 tbsp) milk
90 ml (6 tbsp) cooking oil
1 egg

❶ Sift dry ingredients together. Add spinach, raw bacon and grated cheese and mix slightly.

❷ Beat milk, oil and egg together, and stir into dry ingredients. Mix until flour is moistened; batter should still be lumpy. Spoon into greased muffin tins, filling each two-thirds full.

❸ Bake in a preheated oven at 190 °C (375 °F/gas 5) for 15–20 minutes.

❹ Serve hot with butter.

Makes 12

TIPS

Rinse spinach several times in cold water. Cook in a pan without adding any water. The water left clinging to the leaves is sufficient. Cover tightly and cook until just wilted. Drain, refresh under cold running water, then squeeze well to remove as much moisture as possible.

Substitute fresh spinach with frozen, but drain off excess water.

CHEESE AND CHIVE MUFFINS

1 egg
200 ml (6½ fl oz) milk
150 g (5 oz) plain flour
10 ml (2 tsp) baking powder
2.5 ml (½ tsp) dry mustard
2.5 ml (½ tsp) cayenne pepper
180 g (6 oz) Cheddar cheese, grated
45 ml (3 tbsp) snipped chives

❶ In a measuring jug, beat egg lightly with a fork, then fill jug with milk to 250 ml (8 fl oz) measure.

❷ Sift dry ingredients together, add cheese and chives, and mix in liquid until flour is moistened; batter should still be lumpy.

❸ Spoon into greased muffin tins, filling each two-thirds full. Bake in a preheated oven at 200 °C (400 °F/gas 6) for 15 minutes, until golden brown.

❹ Serve hot with butter.

Makes 8

VARIATIONS

Add 45 ml (3 tbsp) chopped parsley and/or onion to mixture.

Add 75 ml (5 tbsp) chopped bacon, ham or frankfurters to mixture.

TIP

Cayenne pepper is a hot spice ground from red peppers and should be used sparingly. It can be used in curries, soups, sauces and dressings.

Clockwise from top: Cheese and Chive Muffins, Spinach Muffins, Lemon Muffins and Date and Walnut Muffins.

7

BREADS

As more and more people are adopting a healthy way of living, there is an increasing demand for bread recipes using wholemeal flour and bran. Naturally, quick-and-easy recipes are always popular, too. This chapter provides a selection of recipes that satisfy both requirements, and also includes a few for white bread and some interesting variations.

To use yeast successfully it is necessary to know how to use it, and the differences between the various types of yeast.

Instant dry yeast has been used in the recipes in this book because it is easy to use and is the only kind of yeast that is added directly to the dry ingredients. It is also convenient as it reduces rising time, and it's not necessary to dissolve it beforehand.

Instant dry yeast can be purchased in sachets. Once the sachet has been opened, the yeast will deteriorate and should therefore be used immediately. Sealed sachets of dry yeast can be stored in a cool, dry place for up to 18 months.

Active dry yeast and fresh compressed yeast are also available – 10 g (⅓ oz) instant dry yeast is equivalent to one 25 g (¾ oz) cube fresh yeast.

Kneading

This is the most important process in bread making. A good kneading technique is essential as this develops the protein, which is known as gluten, in the flour. As a result of kneading and stretching, the dough becomes elastic, which enables it to rise well and ensures that the product holds its shape.

Before beginning, lightly flour your hands and work surface. Use the palm of your hand to fold the dough repeatedly, working from the outside to the inside. If the dough becomes sticky, sprinkle it with a little flour, but avoid adding too much.

The amount of flour specified in a recipe is only a guide and may vary according to the humidity and the moisture content of the flour used.

Knead for up to 10 minutes, until the dough is smooth and elastic without being sticky. This can also be done successfully using the dough hook of an electric mixer.

Rising

Place the dough in a greased container and cover with cling film or a damp cloth – this helps to retain moisture and prevents a thick skin from forming on the dough. Rising time will depend on temperature; the dough should double in size during rising. The dough will rise best in a warm, humid, draught-free place. To test whether dough has risen properly, press a finger into it. If the dough has risen sufficiently, the impression made by your finger should remain.

Knocking down

After it has risen, turn dough on to a floured surface and knead until it returns to its original volume. This will distribute the air bubbles that have developed throughout the dough during rising, and ensures an even texture. Knock down by pressing the knuckles repeatedly into the risen dough, then shape the dough as desired. If making bread, fill half to two-thirds of tin with dough, placing the fold underneath. Brush bread or rolls with water and leave in a warm place to rise (or prove) once more, covering with cling film or a damp towel as for the first rising; leave to double in size once more.

Glazing

Glazing involves brushing the dough before baking with a glaze such as beaten egg or milk to protect the crust and improves the appearance of the bread. After glazing, sprinkle with seeds, nuts, crushed wheat or rolled oats. One can further improve the appearance of the baked bread by making shallow cuts across the top of the dough with a sharp knife or a pair of scissors, diagonally or in any other pattern.

Baking

Bread is usually baked at about 200 °C (400 °F/gas 6). The high temperature destroys the yeast and stops its action.

Once cooked, the crust should have a good, rich colour. To test whether the loaf is baked, tap its base with your knuckles. If it sounds hollow, it is done. Cool on a wire rack.

Freezing

When completely cooled, wrap bread in cling film and freeze for up to 3 months. Thaw at room temperature for 4–6 hours, or defrost in a microwave oven. Wrap in a damp paper towel and defrost on Medium-low or 30 % power for 4 minutes, depending on size.

QUICK HEALTH BREAD

600 g (1¼ lb) granary flour
5 ml (1 tsp) salt
10 g (⅓ oz) instant dry yeast
15 ml (1 tbsp) sesame seeds
15 ml (1 tbsp) poppy seeds
30 ml (2 tbsp) sunflower seeds
500 ml (16 fl oz) lukewarm water
30 ml (2 tbsp) cooking oil
30 ml (2 tbsp) honey or syrup
seeds or oats for topping

❶ Sift flour and salt together. Add bran left in sieve, yeast and seeds.

❷ Combine water, oil and honey and add to dry ingredients. Mix well.

❸ Spoon into a well-greased 23 cm (9 inch) loaf tin; sprinkle with seeds. Cover lightly with a damp towel and leave to rise in a warm place for 20–30 minutes. Bake bread in a preheated oven at 200 °C (400 °F/gas 6) for 40–45 minutes.

<u>Makes 1 loaf</u>

VARIATION

Bake loaves in tins of different sizes.

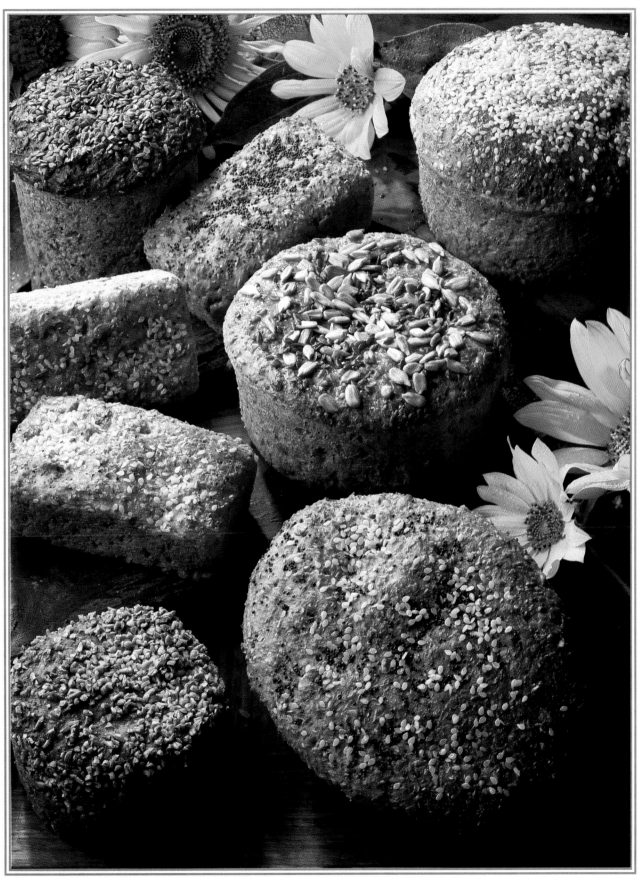

Quick Health Bread.

WHOLEMEAL BREAD

**300 g (9½ oz) Wholemeal flour
280 g (9 oz) plain flour
5 ml (1 tsp) bicarbonate of soda
5 ml (1 tsp) baking powder
5 ml (1 tsp) salt
15 ml (1 tbsp) soft brown sugar
500 ml (16 fl oz) low-fat plain yoghurt
15 ml (1 tbsp) cooking oil
15 ml (1 tbsp) milk
crushed wheat or sesame seeds for topping**

❶ Sift dry ingredients together and add bran left in sieve. Add sugar.

❷ Add yoghurt and oil. Add milk to empty yoghurt container, shake and add to mixture. Mix thoroughly.

❸ Spoon into a greased 23 cm (9 inch) loaf tin and sprinkle with crushed wheat or sesame seeds.

❹ Bake in a preheated oven at 180 °C (350 °F/gas 4) for 45 minutes. Turn off the oven and leave bread inside for a further 15 minutes.

Makes 1 loaf

SEED LOAF

**150 g (5 oz) white bread flour
600 g (1¼ lb) granary flour
10 ml (2 tsp) salt
200 g (6½ oz) crushed wheat
10 g (⅓ oz) instant dry yeast
45 ml (3 tbsp) soft brown sugar
45 ml (3 tbsp) sesame seeds
60 ml (4 tbsp) poppy seeds
45 ml (3 tbsp) linseeds
10 ml (2 tsp) caraway seeds
50 g (2 oz) chopped nuts, mixed
45 ml (3 tbsp) cooking oil
1 litre (1¾ pints) lukewarm water
extra seeds for topping**

❶ Sift plain flour, granary flour and salt together. Add bran left behind in sieve and crushed wheat.

❷ Add yeast, sugar, seeds and nuts.

❸ Mix oil and lukewarm water together, then add to dry ingredients, mixing well.

❹ Spoon into two well-greased 23 cm (9 inch) loaf tins and sprinkle with seeds. Cover lightly with a damp towel and leave to rise in a warm place for 20–30 minutes. Bake in a preheated oven at 200 °C (400 °F/gas 6) for 1 hour.

Makes 2 loaves

TIP

If the water used for activating yeast is too hot, the yeast is killed; too cold, and it is not activated. Achieve the right temperature by mixing one-third boiling with two-thirds cold water.

ONION AND CHEESE BREAD

**500 g (1 lb) self-raising flour
1 packet thick white OR brown onion soup powder
500 ml (16 fl oz) buttermilk
60 g (2 oz) Cheddar cheese, grated
about 15 ml (1 tbsp) milk
pinch of cayenne pepper**

❶ Mix flour, soup powder, buttermilk and half of the cheese together. Add milk to empty buttermilk container, shake, and add to mixture.

❷ Spoon into a lined and greased 23 cm (9 inch) loaf tin and sprinkle remaining cheese and cayenne on top.

❸ Bake in a preheated oven at 180 °C (350 °F/gas 4) for 1 hour.

Makes 1 loaf

VARIATION

SAVOURY BREAD

Add 125 g (4 oz) chopped ham or raw rindless bacon to the ingredients.

TIP

Buttermilk, made by adding a bacterial culture to low-fat or skimmed milk, is more suitable for baking than soured milk.

CHEESE AND HERB TWIST

**470 g (15 oz) brown bread flour
7.5 ml (1½ tsp) salt
10 g (⅓ oz) instant dry yeast
45 ml (3 tbsp) cooking oil
about 340 ml (11 fl oz) lukewarm water
250 g (8 oz) Cheddar cheese OR mozzarella cheese, grated
45 ml (1 tbsp) chopped fresh herbs OR 15 ml (1 tbsp) mixed dried herbs
10 ml (2 tsp) crushed fresh garlic, optional**

❶ Sift flour and salt together, adding bran left in sieve. Mix in dry yeast.

❷ Add oil and lukewarm water and mix to a soft dough.

❸ Turn on to a lightly floured surface and knead dough for 10 minutes, until smooth and elastic. Place dough in an oiled bowl, cover, and allow to rest for 20 minutes.

❹ Knock down the dough and roll out into a rectangle of 30 cm x 35 cm (12 x 14 inches).

❺ Sprinkle cheese, herbs and garlic over. Roll up from short side.

❻ Hold ends of roll and twist in opposite directions. Place on a greased baking tray.

❼ Slash six times across the top and allow to rise for 30–40 minutes.

❽ Bake in a preheated oven at 200 °C (400 °F/gas 6) for 40 minutes. Serve hot.

Makes 1 loaf

Clockwise from top left: Onion and Cheese Bread, Seed Loaf, Wholemeal Bread and Cheese and Herb Twist.

BEER AND CHEESE BREAD

500 g (1 lb) self-raising flour
5 ml (1 tsp) salt
340 ml (11 fl oz) beer
60 g (2 oz) Cheddar cheese, grated
about 30 ml (2 tbsp) water

❶ Place all ingredients in a mixing bowl, reserving half of cheese for topping, and mix together well. Add water if necessary.

❷ Spoon into a lined and greased 23 cm (9 inch) loaf tin and sprinkle remaining cheese on top.

❸ Bake in a preheated oven at 180 °C (350 °F/gas 4) for 1 hour. Serve hot, with butter.

Makes 1 loaf

VARIATION

Replace cheese with 60 g (2 oz) grated bresaola, and add 30 ml (2 tbsp) chopped fresh herbs or 10 ml (2 tsp) dried herbs.

WHITE BREAD

1 kg (2 lb) white bread flour
10 ml (2 tsp) salt
10 ml (2 tsp) caster sugar
10 g (⅓ oz) instant dry yeast
20 ml (4 tsp) margarine
about 625 ml (1 pint) lukewarm water

❶ Sift flour, salt and sugar together. Add dry yeast and mix.

❷ Rub margarine into dry ingredients and gradually add lukewarm water to mix to a soft dough. Add more water if needed.

❸ Turn out on to a lightly floured surface and knead dough for about 10 minutes, until smooth and elastic. Place dough in an oiled bowl, cover, and allow to rest for 20 minutes.

❹ Knock down the dough and divide into two. Place each portion in a greased 23 cm (9 inch) loaf tin, cover with oiled cling film, and leave to rise in a warm place for 30–40 minutes, until double in size.

❺ Brush top with water and bake in a preheated oven at 200 °C (400 °F/gas 6) for 35 minutes.

Makes 2 loaves

TIP

To test whether bread is done, turn it upside down after baking and tap the bottom with your knuckles. If it sounds hollow, it is baked.

VARIATIONS

BROWN BREAD

Follow recipe for white bread, but replace white bread flour with brown bread flour.

POT BREAD

Follow recipe for white bread, but increase the amount of margarine to 60 g (2 oz). After the first rising, knock down, form the dough into one large round loaf, and place in a greased heavy-based pot. Cover and allow to rise until double in volume. Brush with milk or beaten egg. Bake for 45–50 minutes.

FRIED BREAD ROLLS

Follow recipe for white bread, but increase the amount of margarine to 60 g (2 oz). After first rising, knock down and divide dough into 36 pieces. Cover and allow to rise until double in volume. Fry in hot oil.

BARBECUE BREAD

Follow recipe for Fried Bread Rolls, but cook over barbecue on a grid or On a griddle pan on the hob. Do not put oil in the pan.

BONFIRE BREAD

Follow recipe for Fried Bread Rolls, but when dividing dough, make bigger balls. Place balls in warm ashes, but not directly on the coals. Leave for 30 minutes, then remove.

BREAD STICKS (GRISSINI)

Follow recipe for white bread, but increase the amount of margarine to 60 g (2 oz). After the first rising, knock down and divide dough into sticks about 13 cm (5 inches) long. Place on a greased baking tray. Brush with milk or beaten egg; sprinkle with coarse salt, sesame seeds or poppy seeds. Cover and leave to rise until double in volume. Bake at 220 °C (425 °F/gas 7) for 12–15 minutes, until golden and crisp. Store in an airtight container.

BREAD KEBABS

Follow recipe for white bread. After the first rising, knock down and divide dough into 12 even portions. Roll into long sausages and roll around 12 skewers. Barbecue over cooled coals until done. Remove skewers and fill holes with butter and syrup.

FOCCACIA

This is a savoury Italian flat bread, which can be flavoured with fresh herbs and garlic if desired.

1 quantity Pizza Dough (page 14)
45 ml (3 tbsp) olive oil or garlic butter
coarse salt
fresh rosemary or sage, chopped

❶ Follow recipe for pizza dough.

❷ After the first rising, knock down and divide into two rounds. Flatten on greased baking tray or two 25 cm (10 inch) pizza pans.

❸ Brush with olive oil or garlic butter, and sprinkle with salt and rosemary or sage. Cover with cling film and leave to rise in a warm place until double in size – for 15–20 minutes.

❹ Bake in a preheated oven at 200 °C (400 °F/gas 6) for 20 minutes, or until golden brown.

❺ Serve hot, cut into wedges.

Makes 2 loaves

VARIATION

For garlic lovers, crush 4 cloves garlic and sprinkle over dough.

BRAN AND RAISIN LOAF

340 g (11 oz) self-raising flour
2.5 ml (½ tsp) salt
30 g (1 oz) digestive bran
180 g (6 oz) soft brown sugar
90 g (3 oz) seedless raisins
375 ml (12 fl oz) milk

❶ Sift flour and salt together. Mix in all other ingredients.

❷ Pour mixture into a greased and lined 23 cm (9 inch) loaf tin and bake in a preheated oven at 190 °C (375 °F/gas 5) for 50–55 minutes. Serve hot with butter.

Makes 1 loaf

Clockwise from top left: Bran and Raisin Loaf, White Bread, Bread Sticks, Fried Bread Rolls, Foccacia, Barbecue Bread, Bread Kebabs and Pot Bread.

SOFT ROLLS

560 g (1 lb 2 oz) plain flour
5 ml (1 tsp) salt
20 ml (4 tsp) sugar
20 ml (4 tsp) dried milk powder
10 g (⅓ oz) instant dry yeast
30 ml (2 tbsp) margarine
about 250 ml (8 fl oz) lukewarm water
beaten egg or milk to glaze
sesame seeds, poppy seeds or grated cheese for topping

❶ Sift the flour and salt together. Add sugar, milk powder and yeast and mix.

❷ Rub in margarine until mixture resembles fine breadcrumbs.

❸ Add lukewarm water and mix to a soft dough. Turn on to a lightly floured surface and knead for about 10 minutes, until the dough is smooth and elastic.

❹ Place dough in an oiled bowl and cover; allow to rest for 20 minutes.

❺ Knock down dough and divide into 15 equal pieces. Roll each piece into a ball, or shape into long sausages.

❻ Using a rolling pin, roll each ball of dough into a long oval and roll up tightly, like a Swiss roll. Place bread roll, with seam at bottom, on a greased baking tray.

❼ Cover with oiled cling film and allow to rise in a warm place until double in size – 30–40 minutes.

❽ Brush with beaten egg or milk and sprinkle with sesame seeds, poppy seeds or grated cheese.

❾ Bake in a preheated oven at 200 °C (400 °F/gas 6) for 15–20 minutes.

Makes 15

VARIATIONS

SOFT PLAIT

1 Follow recipe for soft rolls. After first rising, knock down dough and divide into two equal pieces.

2 Roll each piece into a 40 cm (16 inch) strand and cross strands in the middle.

3 Take bottom left piece over to top right.

4 Plait the four strands until all the dough has been used. Seal ends together well. Leave to rise in a warm place until double in size – 30–40 minutes. Brush with beaten egg or milk and sprinkle with poppy seeds.

5 Bake in a preheated oven at 200 °C (400 °F/gas 6) for 20–25 minutes.

CROWN LOAF

Place round rolls in a 23 cm (9 inch) loose-bottomed cake tin and sprinkle each with different seeds or cheese. Poppy seeds and sesame seeds are popular for topping bread and rolls, and can also be used in cakes and biscuits.

TIP

The dough will be sticky when you start kneading, but will soon become smooth and satiny. It is properly kneaded when the impression made by a finger remains.

WHOLEMEAL ROLLS

470 g (15 oz) Wholemeal flour
470 g (15 oz) plain flour
10 ml (2 tsp) salt
10 g (⅓ oz) instant dry yeast
15 ml (1 tsp) soft brown sugar, honey or molasses
45 ml (3 tbsp) cooking oil
10 ml (2 tsp) vinegar
about 500 ml (16 fl oz) lukewarm water
beaten egg or milk to glaze

❶ Sift flour and salt together. Add bran left behind in sieve.

❷ Add yeast and brown sugar and combine with dry ingredients.

❸ Mix oil, vinegar and water, add to dry ingredients; mix to a soft dough, adding more water if necessary.

❹ Turn onto a lightly floured surface and knead for about 10 minutes, until the dough is smooth and elastic.

❺ Place dough in an oiled bowl, cover, and allow to rest for 20 minutes.

❻ Knock down the dough and divide into 18 equal pieces. Roll each piece into a ball and shape as desired.

❼ Place rolls on a greased baking tray, cover with oiled cling film, and allow to rise until double in size – roughly 30–40 minutes.

❽ Brush the surface with beaten egg or milk and sprinkle with crushed wheat if desired.

❾ Bake in a preheated oven at 200 °C (400 °F/gas 6) for 20–25 minutes.

Makes 18

TIP

When baking breads with yeast, add a little vinegar to the dough to prevent the 'yeasty' smell that sometimes occurs, especially when too much yeast has been used.

VARIATIONS

HAMBURGER ROLLS

Roll a piece of bread dough into a ball using the palm of the hand.

HOTDOG ROLLS

Using a rolling pin, roll the ball of dough into a long, flat oval and roll up tightly, like a Swiss roll.

CLOVER ROLLS

Divide ball of dough into three equal pieces. Roll each piece into a ball. Join the three balls together to form a triangle.

KNOT ROLLS

Roll ball of dough into a long sausage shape. Make a loop near one end. Thread the remaining piece through the loop and make a knot.

Clockwise from top left: Wholemeal Rolls, Soft Rolls, Soft Plait and Crown Loaf.

8

BISCUITS AND RUSKS

THE WORD 'COOKIE' ORIGINATED FROM THE DUTCH WORD, *KOEKJE*. THE WORD 'BISCUIT' IS DERIVED FROM THE OLD FRENCH WORD, *BESUIT*, A FLAT CAKE OF UNLEAVENED BREAD.
RUSKS ARE DRIED PORTIONS OF BREAD. THEY ARE EASY TO MAKE AND ARE DELICIOUS WHEN PREPARED WITH FLAVOURED DOUGH. TRY ADDING ANISEED OR RAISINS TO YOUR DOUGH MIXTURE.

BISCUITS

Sweet or savoury biscuits are quick and easy to make at home.

According to the way in which they are made, biscuits can be divided into five categories:

Dropped biscuits

The dough is dropped or spooned on to the baking tray as it is very moist and sticky.

Rolled biscuits

The dough used for rolled biscuits is firm and can therefore be rolled out thinly, to a thickness of 3–5 mm (⅛–¼ inch). Cut into shapes with biscuit cutters.

When rolling out, avoid having too much flour on your work surface, as the dough will lose its elasticity. Roll in one direction only to produce an even thickness. Roll sticky dough between two sheets of greaseproof paper.

Shaped biscuits

The dough is forced through a piping bag fitted with a tube, or is shaped by hand or using a biscuit press. The dough must not be too soft or it will not hold its shape. It may be chilled for a while before baking to preserve its shape.

Refrigerator biscuits

The dough is formed into long sausage shapes and chilled in the refrigerator before being cut into slices, arranged on a baking tray, and baked.

Bars or slices

In texture, these resemble cakes, and are baked in cake tins and, once cooled, cut into bars or slices.

Hints on making biscuits

● Ingredients used for making biscuits should be kept at room temperature.

● The resulting number of biscuits will depend on the thickness of the dough when rolled out and on the size of the biscuit cutter.

● The amount of liquid required will depend on the moisture content of the flour.

● Grease baking trays to prevent biscuits from sticking to the tray during baking. Place delicate mixtures on greaseproof paper or rice paper. Baking trays may also be dusted with flour after greasing.

● Remember that most biscuit mixtures spread during baking. When placing mixture on tray, leave sufficient room for spreading.

● Preheat oven before baking.

● Bake biscuits on the middle or top shelf of the oven.

● Once the baking tray is in the oven, ensure that there is space on either side, so that the warm air can circulate.

● If using a conventional oven it is best to bake one sheet of biscuits at a time. If more than one baking tray is placed in the oven at a time, rotate the baking trays half-way through the baking process.

● Biscuits usually bake quickly. A moderate temperature is normally used over a short baking time. Use a timer and check the biscuits frequently to prevent browning or burning.

● Biscuits will be soft when removed from the oven, but will harden during cooling. The longer you bake biscuits, the harder they will become.

Cooling and storing biscuits

Using a spatula, lift biscuits from baking tray immediately after removing from oven to prevent further cooking. Place on a wire rack to cool.

Biscuits should be cooled completely before being stored in an airtight container, which will prevent them from becoming soft. Soft and crisp biscuits should be stored separately. If biscuits become soft, place in a cool oven at 150 °C (300 °F/gas 2) for 5 minutes to restore crispness.

Hard biscuits can be successfully frozen for 2–3 months. Place cold biscuits in a plastic bag or container and store in freezer. When required, allow biscuits to defrost at room temperature.

FLORENTINES

125 g (4 oz) butter
400 g (13 oz) granulated sugar
45 ml (3 tbsp) golden syrup
75 g (2½ oz) plain flour
125 g (4 oz) mixed peel, chopped
125 g (4 oz) glacé cherries, chopped
110 g (3½ oz) nibbed almonds
75 ml (5 tbsp) flaked almonds
110 g (3½ oz) plain cooking chocolate

❶ Melt butter, sugar and syrup together and bring to the boil.

❷ Remove from heat and stir in flour, fruit and nuts.

❸ Place teaspoonfuls of mixture on a lightly greased baking tray, leaving enough space for spreading.

❹ Bake in preheated oven at 160 °C (325 °F/gas 3) for 10–12 minutes.

❺ Remove from oven and smooth rough edges with spatula. When biscuits feel more firm, lift gently from tray; turn on to a wire rack to cool.

❻ Melt chocolate in bowl over hot water and cool until slightly thickened. Spread base of cold biscuits with chocolate. When almost set, create a wavy effect in the chocolate using a fork. Store in the refrigerator.

Makes 50

Florentines.

PECAN BISCUITS

125 g (4 oz) butter or margarine
150 g (5 oz) self-raising flour
75 g (2½ oz) pecan nuts, chopped
2.5 ml (½ tsp) vanilla extract
45 ml (3 tbsp) icing sugar
icing sugar for dusting

❶ Mix together all ingredients, except icing sugar for dusting.

❷ Shape into small balls and place on a greased baking tray. Press down lightly with a fork.

❸ Bake in a preheated oven at 160 °C (325 °F/gas 3) for 25 minutes. Remove from oven and, while still hot, dust with icing sugar. Cool and store in an airtight container.

Makes 20

CINNAMON SNACKS

125 g (4 oz) margarine
75 g (2½ oz) brown sugar
1 egg
5 ml (1 tsp) vanilla extract
165 g (5½ oz) brown bread flour

TOPPING
45 ml (3 tbsp) brown sugar
5 ml (1 tsp) ground cinnamon

❶ Cream the margarine and sugar together. Add egg and extract and beat until light and fluffy.

❷ Add sifted flour and mix to form a soft dough.

❸ For topping: Mix the sugar and cinnamon together.

❹ Shape dough into balls and roll to coat in topping.

❺ Place balls on a baking tray and press down lightly with a fork. Bake in a preheated oven at 180 °C (350 °F/gas 4) for 10–12 minutes. Store biscuits in an airtight container.

Makes 20

CHOCOLATE GINGER BISCUITS

125 g (4 oz) margarine
125 g (4 oz) soft brown sugar
1 egg
210 g (7 oz) brown bread flour
10 ml (2 tsp) baking powder
45 ml (3 tbsp) cocoa powder
90 g (3 oz) crystallized ginger, finely chopped
30 g (1 oz) plain cooking chocolate

❶ Cream margarine and sugar well. Add egg and beat until light and fluffy.

❷ Sift the flour, baking powder and cocoa powder together and add, with bran left behind in sieve, to the creamed mixture.

❸ Add ginger and knead until mixture forms a soft dough.

❹ Shape 5 ml (1 tsp) portions of mixture into balls and place on lightly greased baking trays. Press the biscuits lightly with a fork. Allow room for spreading.

❺ Bake in a preheated oven at 180 °C (350 °F/gas 4) for 12–15 minutes. Turn on to a wire rack to cool.

❻ Melt the chocolate and drizzle over the cold biscuits. Store biscuits in an airtight container.

Makes 30

TIP

Bake biscuits on a baking tray to ensure even browning, which is not always possible in a deeper baking tin.

CRISPY BISCUITS

125 g (4 oz) margarine
90 g (3 oz) granulated sugar
1 egg
150 g (5 oz) brown bread flour
10 ml (2 tsp) baking powder
110 g (3½ oz) sultanas
45 g (1½ oz) cornflakes, lightly crushed

❶ Beat margarine and sugar together. Add egg and beat well until mixture is light and fluffy.

❷ Sift the flour and baking powder together, adding bran left behind in sieve to creamed mixture.

❸ Add sultanas and mix well.

❹ Drop 5 ml (1 tsp) portions of mixture into cornflakes and roll lightly to coat. Place on lightly greased baking tray, allowing room for spreading.

❺ Bake in a preheated oven at 180 °C (350 °F/gas 4) for 20 minutes. Cool biscuits on a wire rack and store in an airtight container.

Makes 24

TIPS

For freshly baked biscuits at a moment's notice, freeze uncooked biscuits on trays. Once frozen, place in plastic bags, seal and freeze for up to 3 months. Defrost and bake as directed.

Undecorated biscuits that are starting to go soft can be crisped up in a hot oven. Place the biscuits on a baking tray and bake at 190 °C (375 °F/gas 5) for 5 minutes.

From top: Crispy Biscuits, Pecan Biscuits, Chocolate Ginger Biscuits and Cinnamon Snacks.

ROMANY CREAMS

250 g (8 oz) butter
250 g (8 oz) sugar
280 g (9 oz) plain flour
5 ml (1 tsp) baking powder
2.5 ml (½ tsp) salt
125 g (4 oz) desiccated coconut
30 ml (2 tbsp) cocoa powder
125 ml (4 fl oz) boiling water

FILLING
125 g (4 oz) sugar
15 ml (1 tbsp) butter
125 ml (4 fl oz) single cream
60 ml (4 tbsp) milk
5 ml (1 tsp) vanilla extract
about 280 g (9 oz) icing sugar
45 g (1½ oz) cooking chocolate, melted, optional

❶ Cream butter and sugar together until light and fluffy.

❷ Sift flour, baking powder and salt and add, with coconut, to creamed mixture. Mix well.

❸ Dissolve cocoa powder in boiling water and add, mixing well.

❹ Roll into balls or place 5 ml (1 tsp) portions on a greased baking tray. Bake in a preheated oven at 180 °C (350 °F/gas 4) for 10–12 minutes.

❺ For filling: Caramelize sugar and butter in a large saucepan.

❻ Remove from heat and add cream and heated milk. Add extract and enough icing sugar to make a spreading consistency. Mix with melted chocolate if desired.

❼ Sandwich pairs of biscuits together with filling.

Makes about 30 double biscuits

TIP

Keep unfilled biscuits in a container and, before serving, simply join two biscuits together with melted cooking chocolate.

BISCUITS FOR BISCUIT PRESS

250 g (8 oz) butter
125 g (4 oz) sugar
2 eggs
10 ml (2 tsp) vanilla extract
340 g (11 oz) plain flour
10 ml (2 tsp) baking powder
2.5 ml (½ tsp) salt

❶ Cream butter and sugar together.

❷ Add eggs one at a time, beating well after each addition. Add extract.

❸ Sift dry ingredients together and add to creamed mixture. Mix well.

❹ Place dough in biscuit press and press on to a greased baking tray.

❺ Bake in a preheated oven at 180 °C (350 °F/gas 4) for 10 minutes. Cool and store in an airtight container.

Makes about 80

VARIATIONS

Replace the 10 ml (2 tsp) vanilla extract with 10 ml (2 tsp) orange extract.

CHOCOLATE BISCUITS

Add 30 ml (2 tbsp) cocoa powder to dry ingredients.

TIP

If no biscuit press is available, roll 5 ml (1 tsp) portions of dough in your hands, place on a greased baking tray, and press lightly with a fork.

SEMOLINA BISCUITS

200 g (6½ oz) butter or margarine
60 ml (4 tbsp) caster sugar
280 g (9 oz) plain flour
165 g (5½ oz) semolina
2.5 ml (½ tsp) salt
60 ml (4 tbsp) milk
caster sugar to sprinkle

❶ Cream butter and sugar until light.

❷ Sift dry ingredients together and knead lightly into butter mixture. Add milk if necessary.

❸ Turn out on to a floured board and roll out to a thickness of 5 mm (¼ inch). Cut into rounds with a biscuit cutter and prick with fork.

❹ Place on a greased baking tray and bake in a preheated oven at 180 °C (350 °F/gas 4) for 15–20 minutes.

❺ Sprinkle with caster sugar. Store in an airtight container.

Makes 50

VARIATION

For a lighter biscuit, replace 45 ml (3 tbsp) plain flour with cornflour.

GINGERSNAPS

125 g (4 oz) margarine
250 g (8 oz) sugar
1 egg
125 ml (4 fl oz) ginger syrup
340 g (11 oz) plain flour
5 ml (1 tsp) bicarbonate of soda
7.5 ml (1½ tsp) ground cinnamon
5 ml (1 tsp) ground ginger

❶ Beat margarine and sugar together.

❷ Add egg, beating well until light and fluffy. Mix in syrup.

❸ Sift dry ingredients together, add to egg mixture and knead well to form a dough. Chill for 1 hour.

❹ Roll out on to a lightly floured surface to a thickness of about 3 mm (⅛ inch). Cut with a biscuit cutter and place on a greased baking tray.

❺ Bake in a preheated oven at 180 °C (350 °F/gas 4) for 10 minutes. Cool and store in an airtight container.

Makes about 40

TIP

Crumble gingersnaps and use to add extra flavour and thickening to gravy in meat dishes.

Clockwise from top left: Romany Creams, Semolina Biscuits, Gingersnaps, Caramel Biscuits and Biscuits for Biscuit Press.

CARAMEL BISCUITS

200 g (6½ oz) butter
135 g (4½ oz) sugar
375 g (12 oz) can condensed milk
5 ml (1 tsp) vanilla extract
470 g (15 oz) plain flour
10 ml (2 tsp) baking powder
2.5 ml (½ tsp) salt

❶ Stir half the sugar with 30 ml (2 tbsp) water over low heat until completely dissolved; then boil until golden. Remove from heat. Beat in condensed milk at once.

❷ Cream butter and remaining sugar together until light and fluffy. Add condensed milk mixture and extract, beating well. Sift dry ingredients together and knead well into mixture.

❸ Roll into small balls, place on ungreased baking sheets and flatten with a fork.

❹ Bake in a preheated oven at 180 °C (350 °F/gas 4) for 10–15 minutes. These biscuits burn easily, so watch carefully, checking bases too. Turn on to wire rack to cool.

Makes about 50

VIENNESE BISCUITS

250 g (8 oz) butter
60 ml (4 tbsp) caster sugar
2.5 ml (½ oz) vanilla extract
250 g (8 oz) plain flour
60 ml (4 tbsp) cornflour
2.5 ml (½ tsp) salt
icing sugar

❶ Beat butter and sugar together well. Add extract.

❷ Sift the flour, cornflour and salt together and blend into mixture until it is of a soft consistency.

❸ Spoon into piping bag fitted with a fluted tube.

❹ Pipe ovals, stars, straight lengths or other shapes on to lightly greased baking trays.

❺ Bake at 180 ˚C (350 ˚F/gas 4) for 12–15 minutes, or until light gold in colour.

❻ Dust lightly with icing sugar before serving. Store in an airtight container.

Makes about 40

VARIATIONS

Dip one end of each biscuit into melted plain chocolate.

Dip one end of each biscuit into Passion Fruit Icing (page 66).

Use a star tube to make star-shaped biscuits. When cool, join together with Orange Icing; dust with icing sugar before serving.

ORANGE ICING

5 ml (1 tsp) grated orange rind
25 ml (5 tsp) orange juice
60 g (2 oz) soft butter
180 g (6 oz) icing sugar
Combine ingredients and beat until smooth.

TIP

To pipe biscuits: Hold piping bag upright, close to baking tray. Press gently to shape biscuit. Turn tube to complete shaping and lift sharply.

COCONUT BISCUITS

250 g (8 oz) butter
250 g (8 oz) sugar
3 egg whites
180 g (6 oz) desiccated coconut
75 g (2½ oz) mixed chopped nuts
2.5 ml (½ tsp) grated lemon rind
470 g (15 oz) plain flour

TOPPING
1 egg white, lightly beaten
45 g (1½ oz) coconut
60 ml (4 tbsp) sugar

❶ Cream butter and sugar together.

❷ Beat egg whites until stiff and fold in coconut, nuts and lemon rind. Fold egg white mixture into sugar mixture.

❸ Sift flour and mix thoroughly into creamed ingredients.

❹ Make rolls approximately 3 cm (1¼ inches) in diameter and chill in refrigerator until firm.

❺ For topping: Brush rolls with egg white. Mix coconut and sugar and sprinkle over rolls.

❻ Cut into slices 5 mm (¼ inch) thick. Place on a greased baking tray and bake in a preheated oven at 180 ˚C (350 ˚F/gas 4) for 12–15 minutes. Turn on to wire rack to cool. Store in an airtight container.

Makes 80

TIPS

To brown desiccated coconut: Place fine coconut on greaseproof paper on a baking tray. Place in a cool oven and brown slowly. Allow to cool before using.

Unbroken egg yolks can be stored in the refrigerator covered with water. Drain off water before using.

VARIATION

Substitute 90 g (3 oz) crunchy peanut butter for sprinkle nuts.

PINWHEEL BISCUITS

60 g (2 oz) butter
375 g (12 oz) sugar
2 egg yolks
5 ml (1 tsp) vanilla extract
560 g (1 lb 2 oz) plain flour
15 ml (1 tbsp) baking powder
pinch salt
90 ml (6 tbsp) milk
45 ml (3 tbsp) cocoa powder
45 ml (3 tbsp) water

❶ Beat butter and sugar together. Add egg yolks and beat well. Add extract.

❷ Sift flour, baking powder and salt together and add, with milk, to creamed mixture. Mix to a stiff dough. Add more milk if required.

❸ Divide mixture in two. Mix cocoa powder and water until smooth and add to one portion.

❹ Sprinkle work surface lightly with flour. Roll out both mixtures separately, to a thickness of 3 mm (¼ inch); place one on top of the other and roll up.

❺ Seal in cling film and refrigerate until firm.

❻ Cut 5 mm (¼ inch) thick slices and place on greased baking trays.

❼ Bake in a preheated oven at 180 ˚C (350 ˚F/gas 4) for 12–15 minutes.

❽ Turn on to a wire rack to cool. Store in an airtight container.

Makes 40, depending on size

TIP

Flour surface to make sure that the dough is not sticky when rolling up.

Clockwise from top right: Coconut Biscuits, Pinwheel Biscuits and Viennese Biscuits.

FRUIT SLICES

150 g (5 oz) self-raising flour
5 ml (1 tsp) mixed spice
125 g (4 oz) caster sugar
150 g (5 oz) mixed dried fruit
45 g (1½ oz) desiccated coconut
110 g (3½ oz) chocolate chips
2 eggs, beaten
110 g (3½ oz) butter, melted

ORANGE ICING
280 g (9 oz) icing sugar
5 ml (1 tsp) soft butter
about 30 ml (2 tbsp) orange juice

❶ Combine sifted dry ingredients, sugar, mixed dried fruit, coconut and chocolate chips.

❷ Stir in eggs and butter. Spoon and press mixture evenly into a greased 20 x 25 cm (8 x 10 inch) rectangular baking tin.

❸ Bake in a preheated oven at 180 °C (350 °F/gas 4) for 20–25 minutes.

❹ Leave to cool for 15 minutes.

❺ For icing: Sift icing sugar, add butter and orange juice and mix until smooth. Spread icing over and leave to cool in tin before cutting into slices. Store in an airtight container.

Makes about 30

SHORTBREAD

500 g (1 lb) butter
180 g (6 oz) icing sugar
560 g (1 lb 2 oz) plain flour
60 ml (4 tbsp) cornflour
pinch salt

❶ Beat the butter and icing sugar together well.

❷ Add the sifted dry ingredients and mix well.

❸ Knead dough very well until smooth, then press flat into an ungreased 20 x 25 cm (8 x 10 inch) rectangular tin. Prick with a fork.

❹ Place in preheated oven at 140 °C (275 °F/gas 1) for 30 minutes and reduce heat to 120 °C (250 °F/gas ½) for another 1½–2 hours.

❺ Cut into fingers while still warm. Leave for a few minutes to cool, then turn out onto a wire rack. Store in an airtight container.

Makes about 30

VARIATION

Divide mixture in two and flatten each into a round shape on an ungreased baking tray using a 20 cm (8 inch) round cake tin as a guide. Use your thumb and forefinger to pinch a decorative border around the edge of the circle. Mark out 12 sections on the shortbread and prick each section with a fork.

NUTTY WHEAT SHORTBREAD

250 g (8 oz) butter
180 g (6 oz) icing sugar
150 g (5 oz) plain flour
60 g (2 oz) cornflour
2.5 ml (½ tsp) salt
150 g (5 oz) granary flour
caster sugar

❶ Beat butter and icing sugar together until light and fluffy.

❷ Add sifted dry ingredients except caster sugar and granary flour to butter mixture. Add bran left in sieve.

❸ Rub in to form a stiff dough.

❹ Press into a 20 x 25 cm (8 x 10 inch) rectangular tin. Prick with a fork and bake in preheated oven at 160 °C (325 °F/gas 3) for 45 minutes.

❺ Leave to cool in tin before cutting into bars. Dust with caster sugar. Store in an airtight container.

Makes 35

CARAMEL SHORTBREAD

SHORTBREAD
125 g (4 oz) butter
125 ml caster sugar
150 g (5 oz) plain flour
25 ml (5 tsp) cornflour
2.5 ml (½ tsp) salt

FUDGE LAYER
75 g (2½ oz) butter
45 ml (3 tbsp) golden syrup
400 g (13 oz) can condensed milk
125 g (4 oz) caster sugar

CHOCOLATE TOPPING
150 g (5 oz) plain chocolate

❶ For shortbread: Beat butter and sugar together until light and fluffy.

❷ Sift the flour, cornflour and salt together and rub into butter and sugar mixture until a stiff dough is formed.

❸ Press into a greased 20 x 25 cm (8 x 10 inch) rectangular tin. Prick with a fork and bake in a preheated oven at 180 °C (350 °F/gas 4) for 10 minutes. Reduce heat to 160 °C (325 °F/gas 3) and bake for a further 10 minutes.

❹ For fudge layer: Boil all ingredients in a saucepan for about 5 minutes, until thick. Beat constantly to prevent burning. Spread over baked shortbread and leave to cool until set.

❺ For chocolate topping: Melt the chocolate in top of double boiler over hot water and spread over fudge layer.

❻ Cut shortbread into squares just before chocolate hardens. Store in an airtight container.

Makes about 50

Clockwise from top left: Crunchies, Caramel Shortbread, Fruit Slices, Nutty Wheat Shortbread and Shortbread.

CRUNCHIES

200 g (6½ oz) margarine
7.5 ml (1½ tsp) bicarbonate
of soda
15 ml (1 tbsp) golden syrup
180 g (6 oz) rolled oats
150 g (5 oz)white bread flour
250 g (8 oz) caster sugar
90 g (3 oz) desiccated coconut

❶ Melt margarine and add bicarbonate of soda and syrup.

❷ Mix dry ingredients together and combine with the melted mixture.

❸ Press into a 20 x 25 cm (8 x 10 inch) rectangular tin and bake in a preheated oven at 160 °C (325 °F/gas 3) for 40-45 minutes, until golden brown.

❹ Remove from oven and cut into squares while still warm. Store in an airtight container.

Makes about 25

VARIATIONS

Substitute plain flour or brown bread flour for the white bread flour.

Replace golden syrup with maple syrup.

TIP

Crunchies will store well in the freezer for 6 months.

PEANUT CARAMEL BARS

125 g (4 oz) butter or margarine
125 g (4 oz) sugar
1 egg yolk
180 g (6 oz) plain flour
2.5 ml (½ tsp) baking powder
25 ml (5 tsp) custard powder
2.5 ml (½ tsp) salt

TOPPING
75 g (2½ oz) soft brown sugar
30 ml (2 tbsp) golden syrup
90 g (3 oz) butter or margarine
75 g (2½ oz) unsalted peanuts

❶ Beat butter and sugar together. Add egg yolk and mix until light and fluffy.

❷ Add dry ingredients and mix to form a stiff dough.

❸ Press mixture into a well-greased 20 x 25 cm (8 x 10 inch) rectangular baking tin.

❹ Bake in a preheated oven at 180 °C (350 °F/gas 4) for 20-25 minutes, or until golden brown.

❺ For topping: Place brown sugar, golden syrup and butter in a saucepan. Stir over a low heat until butter has melted and sugar has dissolved. Simmer gently for 5 minutes. Stir in roughly chopped peanuts.

❻ Remove from the oven, spread with prepared topping mixture, and return to the oven for a further 5 minutes. Leave to cool in the tin, then cut into bars. Store in an airtight container.

Makes about 25

TIP

Butter gives a superior flavour and is responsible for the richness and shortness of the biscuit.

RUSKS

Rusks can be made from white flour or wholemeal flour, which is the more popular because of its health benefit. The rusk dough is shaped into small balls, which are arranged next to one another. Butter or margarine can be used, but butter gives a better flavour than margarine. However, if rusks are to be kept for a long time, margarine is recommended.

After baking, place rusks on a wire rack and break in half using two forks. Some rusks may need to be cut with a knife. Place rusks on a wire rack on an ungreased baking tray and dry out overnight in the warming drawer of the cooker.

Alternatively, dry them in the oven at the lowest temperature until completely dried out. (Place a spoon in the oven door to allow moisture to escape.)

Check rusks to prevent them from burning or becoming too brown. Turn them over and dry on the other side as well. Cool completely before storing in an airtight container. Rusks can be stored this way for up to 3 months.

BRAN RUSKS

800 ml (26 fl oz) boiling water
375 g (12 oz) sugar
340 g (11 oz) margarine
3 eggs, beaten
1 kg (2 lb) self-raising flour
15 ml (1 tbsp) baking powder
10 ml (2 tsp) salt
5 ml (1 tsp) cream of tartar
60 g (2 oz) digestive bran

❶ Combine boiling water, sugar and margarine. Stir until margarine has melted. Allow mixture to cool and add eggs.

❷ Sift flour, baking powder, salt and cream of tartar together, and add to egg mixture.

❸ Add digestive bran and stir until well mixed. (Mixture will be runny.)

❹ Pour into three greased 23 cm (9 inch) loaf tins.

❺ Bake in a preheated oven at 180 °C (350 °F/gas 4) for 1 hour.

❻ Leave in tins for a few minutes to cool. Turn out on to a wire rack to cool completely. Cut each loaf into seven thick slices and then divide each slice into three again. (Use an electric knife, if possible, to prevent breaking.)

❼ Dry out overnight in warming drawer, or in a very cool oven.

Makes 72, depending on size

WHOLEMEAL RUSKS

500 g (1 lb) plain flour
500 g (1 lb) granary flour
45 ml (3 tbsp) baking powder
5 ml (1 tsp) salt
250 g (8 oz) sugar
500 g (1 lb) butter
500 ml (16 fl oz) buttermilk

❶ Sift dry ingredients together. Add bran left behind in sieve. Add sugar.

❷ Melt butter and add buttermilk. Mix into dry ingredients.

❸ Shape dough into balls and place in a large, greased oven pan.

❹ Bake in a preheated oven at 180 °C (350 °F/gas 4) for 1 hour.

❺ Break into pieces and dry out in the warming drawer overnight, or in a very cool oven.

Makes 40, depending on size

From top: Wholemeal Rusks, Bran Rusks and Peanut Caramel Bars.

HEALTH RUSKS

500 g (1 lb) margarine
280 g (9 oz) soft brown sugar
2 eggs, beaten
500 ml (16 fl oz) buttermilk
1 kg (2 lb) self-raising flour
15 ml (1 tbsp) baking powder
5 ml (1 tsp) salt
200 g (6½ oz) All Bran Flakes
75 g (2½ oz) digestive bran
60 g (2 oz) sunflower seeds
90 g (3 oz) seedless raisins

❶ Melt margarine and sugar together. Leave to cool.

❷ Add eggs and buttermilk.

❸ Sift flour, baking powder and salt together. Add All Bran Flakes, digestive bran, sunflower seeds and raisins. Add egg mixture.

❹ Shape into balls and place in a large, greased baking tin.

❺ Bake in a preheated oven at 180 °C (350 °F/gas 4) for 45–50 minutes.

❻ Turn out on to a wire rack to cool slightly, break open while still warm, and leave to cool further. Dry out overnight in the warming drawer, or in a very cool oven.

Makes 60, depending on size

TIPS

Do not cut these rusks with a knife as they will break easily.

Place spoon in oven door while drying out to allow air to circulate.

CONDENSED MILK RUSKS

2.5 kg (5½ lb) plain flour
20 ml (4 tsp) salt
400 g (13 oz) sugar
20 g (¾ oz) instant dry yeast
2 eggs, beaten
1.5 litres (2½ pints) lukewarm water
250 g (8 oz) margarine or butter, melted
400 g (13 oz) can condensed milk

❶ Sift flour and salt together. Add sugar and dry yeast.

❷ Mix eggs, lukewarm water, margarine and condensed milk together, add to dry ingredients, and mix to a soft dough.

❸ Knead dough for about 10 minutes, until smooth and elastic.

❹ Place dough in an oiled bowl, cover and leave to rise for 20 minutes.

❺ Knock down the dough and shape into balls. Place in large greased baking tins, cover with oiled cling film, and leave to rise in a warm place until double in size – about 30 minutes.

❻ Bake in a preheated oven at 180 °C (350 °F/gas 4) for 1 hour.

❼ Turn out on to a wire rack to cool slightly, break open while still warm, and leave to cool further. Dry out overnight in the warming drawer, or in a very cool oven.

Makes 200, depending on size

TIP

Cut dough with a pair of kitchen scissors and shape into balls.

BUTTERMILK RUSKS 1

2.5 kg (5½ lb) self-raising flour
10 ml (2 tsp) salt
600 g (1¼ lb) sugar
15 ml (1 tbsp) whole aniseed, optional
725 g (1½ lb) margarine
1.5 litres (2½ pints) buttermilk
3 eggs, beaten

❶ Sift flour and salt together. Add sugar and aniseed. Rub in margarine until mixture resembles breadcrumbs.

❷ Mix buttermilk and eggs together, add to above mixture and mix well.

❸ Shape dough into balls and place in large, greased baking tins.

❹ Bake in a preheated oven at 160 °C (325 °F/gas 3) for 20 minutes and then reduce heat to 150 °C (300 °F/gas 2) for a further 30 minutes.

❺ Turn out on to a wire rack to cool slightly, break open while still warm, and leave to cool further. Dry out overnight in the warming drawer, or in a very cool oven.

Makes 200, depending on size

TIP

If rusks brown too quickly, cover with foil to prevent further browning.

BUTTERMILK RUSKS 2

1.5 kg (3 lb) self-raising flour
2.5 ml (½ tsp) salt
10 ml (2 tsp) cream of tartar
500 g (1 lb) butter
340 g (11 oz) sugar
500 ml (16 fl oz) buttermilk

❶ Sift dry ingredients together.

❷ Melt butter and sugar together and add, together with buttermilk, to dry ingredients. Mix well.

❸ Shape into balls and place in a large greased baking tin.

❹ Bake in a preheated oven at 180 °C (350 °F/gas 4) for 1 hour.

❺ Turn out on to a wire rack to cool slightly, break open while still warm, and leave to cool further. Dry out overnight in the warming drawer, or in a very cool oven.

Makes 40, depending on size

Clockwise from top left: Buttermilk Rusks 2, Condensed Milk Rusks, Buttermilk Rusks 1 and Health Rusks.

9

DESSERTS

'DESSERT' IS DERIVED FROM A FRENCH WORD MEANING 'TO CLEAR THE TABLE', A TRADITION STILL PRACTISED IN RESTAURANTS BEFORE THE SWEET COURSE IS SERVED. NO MATTER WHETHER IT IS CALLED 'DESSERT', 'PUDDING' OR 'SWEET', THIS PART OF THE MEAL IS SOMETHING SPECIAL – FOR SOME, THE BEST PART! THE RECIPES IN THIS CHAPTER CATER FOR EVERY TASTE, AND INCLUDE BAKED AND, BATTER PUDDINGS, ICED DESSERTS, FRUIT PUDDINGS AND A COLD MOUSSE.

VANILLA AND CHOCOLATE ICE-CREAM

250 g (8 oz) sugar
60 ml (4 tbsp) plain flour
2.5 ml (½ tsp) salt
750 ml (1¼ pints) milk
2 eggs
15 ml (1 tbsp) vanilla extract
250 ml (8 fl oz) whipping cream, beaten
90 g (3 oz) plain chocolate

❶ Mix sugar, flour and salt in a heavy-based saucepan. Add milk; bring to boil. Boil for 5 minutes while beating.

❷ Add a little mixture to beaten eggs. Pour into milk and boil until thickened – for 3–5 minutes. Leave to cool.

❸ Add 10 ml (2 tsp) of extract and the cream to cooled custard. Divide mixture in half; add 5 ml (1 tsp) extract to one half for vanilla ice-cream.

❹ Melt chocolate and add to second half. Freeze both halves separately. Serve with chocolate or caramel sauce once frozen.

Makes 1 litre (1¾ pints)

VARIATION

Substitute 10 ml (2 tsp) peppermint extract and a few drops of green food colouring for the vanilla extract.

TUILES

90 g (3 oz) butter
90 g (3 oz) caster sugar
90 g (3 oz) plain flour
1 egg white

❶ Cream butter and sugar together. Add flour and mix well.

❷ Lightly beat egg white and add to creamed mixture.

❸ Place about two teaspoonfuls of mixture on a greased baking tray. Use a spatula or spoon to spread evenly in a large circle.

❹ Bake in a preheated oven at 180 ˚C (350 ˚F/gas 4) for 6–7 minutes, until just starting to brown. Bake only four at a time as they must be shaped immediately after baking, before they set.

❺ Remove carefully with a spatula and place each over the bottom of an inverted glass, pressing lightly. Cool.

❻ Fill with Ice-cream (this page) or Custard (page 98) and serve on top of puréed fruit.

Makes 24

TIPS

These biscuits start getting hard and crisp very quickly, so bake only a few at a time.

APPLE AND PEAR CRUMBLE

375 g (12 oz) can apple pie filling
400 g (13 oz) can pears, drained
90 g (3 oz) raisins
5 ml (1 tsp) ground cinnamon
5 ml (1 tsp) ground ginger
110 g (3½ oz) plain flour
90 g (3 oz) soft brown sugar
60 g (2 oz) margarine

❶ Mix apples, pears, raisins, cinnamon and ginger together; spoon into a 23 cm (9 inch) ovenproof pie dish.

❷ Sift flour and add sugar. Rub in margarine until mixture resembles fine breadcrumbs. Sprinkle over fruit.

❸ Bake in a preheated oven at 180 ˚C (350 ˚F/gas 4) for 30 minutes. Serve with cold, thick fresh cream, custard or ice-cream.

Serves 4-6

PASSION FRUIT CREAM

45 ml (3 tbsp) plain flour
125 g (4 oz) caster sugar
10 ml (2 tsp) gelatine
200 ml (6½ fl oz) water
250 ml (8 fl oz) apricot juice
110 g (3½ oz) can passion fruit pulp
165 g (5½ oz) can evaporated milk, chilled

❶ Combine flour, sugar, gelatine and water in a saucepan. Simmer until mixture thickens, stirring constantly.

❷ Stir in juice and passion fruit pulp. Refrigerate until mixture starts to set.

❸ Beat milk until fluffy and fold into passion fruit mixture.

❹ Pour into serving glasses and refrigerate until set. Serve with cream or ice-cream.

Serves 4

VARIATION

Substitute orange juice for apricot juice.

Clockwise from top left: Apple and Pear Crumble, Passion Fruit Cream and Tuile with Vanilla Ice-cream.

BASIC PANCAKES

280 g (9 oz) plain flour
2.5 ml (½ tsp) salt
2 eggs
500 ml (16 fl oz) water
5 ml (1 tsp) brandy or lemon juice
cinnamon sugar

❶ Sift flour and salt together.

❷ Whisk eggs and water together and add to flour. Add brandy, beating constantly until smooth.

❸ Leave batter to stand for at least an hour before using. If batter is too thick, add more water.

❹ Lightly oil a heavy-based frying pan and heat. Pour batter into pan; fry until lightly browned on both sides.

❺ Sprinkle with cinnamon sugar and roll up.

Makes 15–20, depending on pan size

VARIATION

CREPES
Make crêpes using 150 g (5 oz) plain flour to 2 eggs. Serve with Orange Sauce (this page).

TIPS

Keep pancakes warm by placing over boiling water.

To freeze, leave pancakes to cool, then stack between sheets of grease-proof paper. Wrap in foil and freeze for up to 2 months. To use, thaw and peel off one by one.

To keep crêpes warm, brush with melted butter and place in oven.

Batter can be frozen.

Custard Filling

45 ml (3 tbsp) custard powder
500 ml (16 fl oz) milk
25 ml (5 tsp) sugar
440 g (14 oz) can pineapple pieces, drained
30 g (1 oz) margarine
5 ml (1 tsp) vanilla extract

❶ Mix custard powder with a little milk. Heat remaining milk and sugar.

❷ Stir custard mixture into milk. Cut pineapple into smaller pieces and add. Cook until thickened.

❸ Remove from heat and stir in margarine and extract.

❹ Fill pancakes.

Orange Sauce

125 g (4 oz) sugar
200 ml (6½ fl oz) orange juice
90 g (3 oz) margarine
10 ml (2 tsp) grated orange rind
15 ml (1 tbsp) cornflour
25 ml (5 tsp) brandy

❶ Heat sugar, orange juice, margarine and orange rind. Thicken with cornflour and leave to boil a few minutes.

❷ Heat brandy in a small saucepan (do not boil), pour over sauce, ignite and leave until flames subside.

VARIATION

Substitute Grand Marnier or Tia Maria for brandy.

WHOLEMEAL PANCAKES

150 g (5 oz) plain flour
150 g (5 oz) granary flour
2.5 ml (½ tsp) salt
2 eggs
250 ml (8 fl oz) milk
375 ml (12 fl oz) water
45 ml (3 tbsp) oil
15 ml (1 tbsp) brandy or lemon juice
cinnamon sugar

❶ Sift flours and salt together. Add bran left behind in sieve.

❷ Whisk eggs, milk and water together and add gradually to the dry ingredients, beating constantly.

❸ Add oil and brandy and beat well.

❹ Allow batter to stand, covered, for 1½ hours before using. If batter is too thick, add more water.

❺ Pour a little batter into a lightly oiled and heated heavy-based frying pan. Tip pan to allow mixture to coat base evenly. Fry for 1–2 minutes or until lightly browned.

❻ Turn pancake and fry the other side. Sprinkle with cinnamon sugar and roll up or fill with Almond Filling, and top with Strawberry Sauce.

Makes 15–20 depending on pan size

Almond Filling

125 ml (4 oz) sugar
250 ml (8 fl oz) milk
60 ml (4 tbsp) plain flour
2 eggs, separated
60 ml (4 tbsp) nibbed almonds
45 g (1½ oz) margarine
5 ml (1 tsp) vanilla extract
2.5 ml (½ tsp) almond extract

Strawberry Sauce

400 g (13 oz) can strawberries in syrup
60 ml (4 tbsp) sugar
15 ml (1 tbsp) cornflour

❶ For filling: Heat sugar, milk and flour together. Beat until smooth.

❷ Add some of the hot mixture to beaten egg yolks. Pour into hot mixture, beat well and cook over low heat until mixture starts to thicken.

❸ Remove from heat. Add almonds, margarine and vanilla and almond extracts.

❹ Beat egg whites until stiff and fold into mixture.

❺ For sauce: Heat strawberries with their syrup and the sugar. Thicken with cornflour and water paste and boil for a few minutes.

❻ Fill pancakes, and pour sauce over.

From top: Crêpes with Orange Sauce, Wholemeal Pancakes with Almond Filling and Strawberry Sauce.

SEMOLINA PUDDING

500 ml (16 fl oz) milk
45 ml (3 tbsp) semolina
20 g (¾ oz) margarine
1 egg, separated
2.5 ml (½ tsp) grated lemon rind
45 ml (3 tbsp) caster sugar
extra caster sugar for
sprinkling

❶ Heat milk, add semolina, and simmer for about 5 minutes.

❷ Remove from heat and add margarine, egg yolk, lemon rind and sugar.

❸ Beat egg white until soft peak stage. Gently fold into egg mixture and pour into a 20 cm (8 inch) round ovenproof dish.

❹ Sprinkle extra caster sugar over and bake in a preheated oven at 180 °C (350 °F/gas 4) for 20 minutes.

Serves 4

TIP

Never waste rind. Grate off before halving and squeezing the fruit; store in a covered container in the freezer. Use in frozen state.

CHOCOLATE SELF-SAUCING PUDDING

45 g (1½ oz) butter or margarine
200 g (6½ oz) caster sugar
1 egg
150 g (5 oz) plain flour
25 ml (5 tsp) cocoa powder
15 ml (1 tbsp) baking powder
2.5 ml (½ tsp) salt
200 ml (6½ fl oz) milk

SYRUP
250 ml (8 fl oz) water
150 g (5 oz) soft brown sugar
25 ml (5 tsp) cocoa powder
5 ml (1 tsp) vanilla extract

❶ Cream butter and sugar. Add egg and beat until light and fluffy.

❷ Sift dry ingredients and add, alternately with milk, to butter mixture.

❸ Spoon the mixture into a large ovenproof dish.

❹ For syrup: Mix all ingredients except extract in a saucepan, heat and stir until sugar has dissolved and mixture starts to boil. Add extract.

❺ Pour syrup over batter and bake in a preheated oven at 180 °C (350 °F/gas 4) for 30 minutes. Serve with custard or fresh cream.

Serves 4–6

MERINGUE PUDDING

15 g (½ oz) margarine
125 g (4 oz) sugar
2 eggs, separated
150 g (5 oz) plain flour
5 ml (1 tsp) baking powder
2.5 ml (½ tsp) salt
500 ml (16 fl oz) milk
45 ml (3 tbsp) sieved apricot jam
25 ml (5 tsp) sugar for egg whites

❶ Cream the margarine and sugar together. Add egg yolks and beat until light and fluffy.

❷ Sift flour, baking powder and salt and add, alternately with 90 ml (6 tbsp) milk, to sugar mixture.

❸ Spoon into a greased ovenproof dish and bake in a preheated oven at 180 °C (350 °F/gas 4) for 40 minutes.

❹ Remove from oven and pour remaining milk over pudding. Spread apricot jam over.

❺ Beat egg whites with 25 ml (5 tsp) sugar until soft peak stage. Spread over pudding and bake for a further 15 minutes, until golden brown. Serve with custard.

Serves 6

LEMON PUDDING

75 g (2½ oz) plain flour
2.5 ml (½ tsp) salt
200 g (6½ oz) sugar
45 g (1½ oz) butter or margarine
3 eggs, separated
10 ml (2 tsp) grated lemon rind
60 ml (4 tbsp) lemon juice
250 ml (8 fl oz) milk

❶ Sift flour and salt together. Add sugar.

❷ Rub in butter until mixture resembles fine breadcrumbs.

❸ Beat in egg yolks, lemon rind, lemon juice and milk until smooth.

❹ Fold in stiffly beaten egg whites.

❺ Pour into a medium-sized, greased ovenproof dish and place in baking tin or roasting pan half-filled with water. Bake in a preheated oven at 180 °C (350 °F/gas 4) for 35 minutes.

Serves 4

TIPS

Before grating lemon rind, dip grater into cold water. The rind will slip off the grater more easily.

When a small amount of lemon juice is needed, make a hole in the lemon with a skewer and squeeze out the amount required. Store lemon in the refrigerator.

To create a delicate texture, place a layer of newspaper in the water under the dish during baking.

Clockwise from top left: Meringue Pudding, Chocolate Self-saucing Pudding, Semolina Pudding and Lemon Pudding.

PINEAPPLE UPSIDE-DOWN PUDDING

125 g (4 oz) butter
75 ml (5 tbsp) soft brown sugar
440 g (14 oz) can pineapple rings
glacé cherries
pecan nuts
200 g (6½ oz) caster sugar
1 egg
210 g (7 oz) self-raising flour
2.5 ml (½ tsp) salt
125 ml (4 fl oz) milk

❶ Grease base of a 20 cm (8 inch) cake tin or medium-sized ovenproof dish.

❷ Cream 60 g (2 oz) of butter with brown sugar and spoon on to base of tin. Place pineapple rings on base and decorate with cherries and nuts.

❸ Cream the remaining butter with the caster sugar. Add egg and beat until light and fluffy.

❹ Sift flour and salt together and add, alternately with milk, to egg mixture.

❺ Spoon mixture over fruit and bake in a preheated oven at 180 °C (350 °F/gas 4) for 40–50 minutes.

❻ Turn out on to a serving dish and serve hot with ice-cream or cream.

Serves 6

TIP

If you are using an ovenproof dish, place extra pineapple rings around sides of dish.

101

PEACH STRUDEL

PASTRY
150 g (5 oz) plain flour
2.5 ml (½ oz) salt
30 g (1 oz) melted butter
1 egg yolk
about 60 ml (4 tbsp) lukewarm water
extra butter, melted

FILLING
15 g (½ oz) butter
30 g (1 oz) fresh breadcrumbs
400 g (13 oz) can peach slices in syrup,
drained
90 g (3 oz) sugar
10 ml (2 tsp) ground cinnamon
2.5 ml (½ tsp) allspice
90 g (3 oz) seedless raisins

❶ For pastry: Sift flour and salt together. Make a well in centre and mix in half of melted butter.

❷ Mix egg yolk and water together and add to dry ingredients. Mix to form a soft dough. Beat until dough comes away from sides of bowl.

❸ Knead well, until smooth and elastic. Flatten dough and brush with remaining melted butter. Cover well and leave to stand at room temperature for at least 30 minutes or overnight if possible. Dough will become more elastic.

❹ Place dough on surface sprinkled with flour and roll out very thinly. Stretch while rolling out to a very thin rectangular shape of about 25 x 35 cm (10 x 14 inches). Brush pastry with melted butter.

❺ For filling: Heat butter and fry breadcrumbs until crisp. Spread over pastry.

❻ Combine peach slices with sugar, cinnamon, allspice and raisins.

❼ Place filling on one edge of pastry. Starting from this end, roll up tightly.

❽ Place on greased baking tray and brush with remaining melted butter.

❾ Bake in a preheated oven at 190 ℃ (375 ℉/gas 5) for 30-35 minutes.

❿ Cut into diagonal slices; serve hot.

Serves 6

VARIATION

Substitute canned apples, cherries or apricots for peaches.

TIP

Freeze strudel unbaked. To bake, place, frozen, in a preheated oven and bake as directed in recipe, allowing an extra 15–20 minutes baking time.

BAKED ROLY-POLY

280 g (9 oz) self-raising flour
pinch salt
125 g (4 oz) butter
2 eggs
45 ml (3 tbsp) milk
2.5 ml (½ tsp) vanilla extract
75 ml (5 tbsp) sieved apricot jam

SYRUP
375 ml (12 fl oz) boiling water
250 g (8 oz) sugar
30 g (1 oz) butter

❶ Sift flour and salt together. Rub in butter until the mixture resembles breadcrumbs.

❷ Beat eggs, milk and extract, stir into flour, and mix to a soft dough.

❸ On floured surface, roll out dough to a thickness of 5 mm (¼ inch) and a rectangular shape of about 23 x 25 cm (9 x 10 inches). Spread with jam.

❹ Roll up as for Swiss roll, cut into slices of 2 cm (¾ inch), and place in a rectangular ovenproof dish.

❺ For syrup: Mix all ingredients together and pour over slices.

❻ Bake in a preheated oven at 180 ℃ (350 ℉/gas 4) for 30–45 minutes.

Serves 4-6

SPICY DUMPLINGS

150 g (5 oz) plain flour
2.5 ml (½ tsp) salt
5 ml (1 tsp) bicarbonate of soda
15 g (½ oz) margarine
1 egg, beaten
30 ml (2 tbsp) milk
15 ml (1 tbsp) sieved apricot jam

SYRUP
375 ml (12 fl oz) water
250 g (8 oz) sugar
5 ml (1 tsp) ground cinnamon
5 ml (1 tsp) ground ginger
2.5 ml (½ tsp) ground nutmeg

❶ Sift flour, salt and bicarbonate of soda together. Rub in margarine.

❷ Add egg, milk and apricot jam and mix well.

❸ For syrup: Mix all ingredients together and bring to the boil.

❹ Drop spoonfuls of dough into the boiling syrup. Cover and boil for 15 minutes. Do not remove the lid while cooking. Serve hot.

Serves 4

TRIFLE

1 Swiss roll (page 56)
sieved apricot jam
125 ml (4 fl oz) sherry
400 g (13 oz) can peach slices in syrup,
drained
45 g (1½ oz) halved glacé cherries
60 g (2 oz) walnuts, optional
1 quantity Confectioner's Custard
(page 43)
125 ml (4 fl oz) fresh cream, whipped

❶ Cut cake into slices and place in serving dish. Sprinkle with sherry and leave to soak while preparing custard.

❷ Arrange fruit, cherries and nuts on soaked cake. Cover with custard. Extra fruit can be placed on top of cake if desired.

❸ Decorate with whipped cream, extra cherries and nuts. Chill for a few hours, or overnight if possible.

Serves 6-8

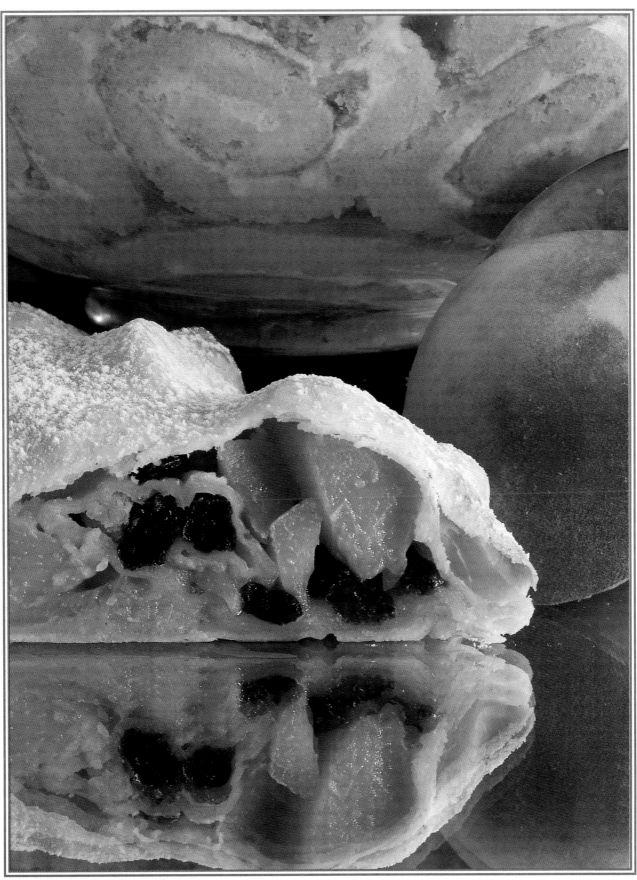

From top: Trifle and Peach Strudel.

10

BAKING FOR SPECIAL OCCASIONS

EASTER IS CELEBRATED IN DIFFERENT WAYS ALL OVER THE WORLD AND VARIOUS SPECIAL FOODS ARE ASSOCIATED WITH IT. FOR EXAMPLE, HOT CROSS BUNS, DECORATED WITH THE SYMBOLIC CROSS, ARE CUSTOMARILY EATEN ON GOOD FRIDAY. SPICE BUNS, WHICH ARE SIMILAR, ARE ALSO EATEN AT EASTER. CHRISTMAS IS USUALLY A TIME OF JOY AND EXCHANGING PRESENTS. MINCE PIES OR INDIVIDUAL CHRISTMAS CAKES ARE ALWAYS POPULAR GIFTS.

HOT CROSS BUNS

375 ml (¾ pint) milk
60 g (2 oz) butter
560 g (1 lb 2 oz) plain flour
15 ml (1 tbsp) mixed spice
5 ml (1 tsp) ground cinnamon
5 ml (1 tsp) salt
60 ml (4 tbsp) caster sugar
10 g (⅓ oz) instant dry yeast
150 g (5 oz) sultanas
1 egg, beaten

FLOUR PASTE FOR CROSSES
75 g (2½ oz) plain flour
10 ml (2 tsp) caster sugar
about 75 ml (5 tbsp) water

GLAZE
30 ml (2 tbsp) milk
30 ml (2 tbsp) caster sugar

❶ Heat milk and butter together and leave to cool slightly.

❷ Sift flour, spices and salt together. Add sugar, yeast and sultanas.

❸ Stir in warm milk and butter, and egg. Knead well until smooth – about 10 minutes. Cover and leave in a warm place for about 1 hour, or until dough has doubled in size.

❹ Knead a few minutes until smooth. Divide into 12 medium-sized balls and place on a greased baking tray. Cover and leave in a warm place for 10 minutes, or until the buns have risen.

❺ For crosses: Mix flour and sugar together and add enough water to form a smooth paste. Place the paste in a piping bag; using the small, plain tube, make crosses on the buns.

❻ Bake in a preheated oven at 190 ˚C (375 ˚F/gas 5) for 15–20 minutes.

❼ For glaze: Heat milk and sugar without boiling. Turn buns on to a wire rack and brush with hot glaze.

Makes 12

QUICK SPICE MUFFINS

These muffins are similar to Hot Cross Buns, but do not have the same texture. They are popular all year round.

560 g (1 lb 2 oz) plain flour
25 ml (5 tsp) baking powder
2.5 ml (½ tsp) salt
15 ml (1 tbsp) mixed spice
5 ml (1 tsp) cinnamon
200 g (6½ oz) margarine
125 g (4 oz) soft brown sugar
315 g (10 oz) mixed dried fruit
1 egg
375 ml (12 fl oz) milk

❶ Sift dry ingredients together.

❷ Rub in margarine until mixture resembles breadcrumbs.

❸ Add sugar and dried fruit.

❹ Whisk egg and milk together and add to dry ingredients. Mix until flour is moistened; do not over-beat, batter should still be lumpy.

❺ Spoon into greased muffin tins, filling each two-thirds full. Bake in a preheated oven at 190 ˚C (375 ˚F/gas 5) for 20–25 minutes.

❻ Serve with butter.

Makes 24

POPPY SEED EASTER CAKE

200 g (6½ oz) butter
375 ml (12 oz) caster sugar
5 eggs, separated
470 g (15 oz) plain flour
25 ml (5 tsp) baking powder
250 ml (8 fl oz) orange juice
125 ml (4 fl oz) sherry
60 g (2 oz) poppy seeds
125 g (4 oz) caster sugar

❶ Cream butter and sugar together until light and fluffy.

❷ Add egg yolks and beat well.

❸ Add sifted flour and baking powder alternately with the orange juice. Add sherry.

❹ Gradually add the poppy seeds to mixture while beating well.

❺ In a separate bowl, whisk the egg whites and sugar until stiff. Fold egg whites into the poppy seed mixture.

❻ Pour mixture into a greased, deep round or square 23 cm (9 inch) cake tin.

❼ Bake in a preheated oven at 160 ˚C (325 ˚F/gas 3) for 1½ hours. Turn out on to a wire rack to cool.

TIP

For use in cakes, poppy seeds are often ground, or cooked in milk until soft. It is believed that the best poppy seeds, slate-blue in colour, come from the Netherlands. In some countries they are crushed for their oil, which is used as salad oil.

Clockwise from top: Hot Cross Buns, Quick Spice Muffins and Poppy Seed Easter Cake.

SIMNEL CAKE

Today, simnel cake is associated with Easter Sunday, the marzipan balls representing the 11 faithful disciples.

200 g (6½ oz) butter or margarine
90 g (3 oz) soft brown sugar
3 eggs
500 g (1 lb) mixed dried fruit
210 g (7 oz) plain flour
5 ml (1 tsp) ground cinnamon
5 ml (1 tsp) ground mixed spice
2.5 ml (½ tsp) ground nutmeg
2.5 ml (½ tsp) salt
725 g (1½ lb) marzipan
apricot jam for spreading

❶ Cream butter and sugar well.

❷ Add eggs, one at a time. Beat well until light and fluffy.

❸ Add dried fruit and sifted dry ingredients. Mix well.

❹ Grease and line a 18 cm (7 inch) round, 7.5 cm (3 inch) deep cake tin. Spread half of cake mixture on to base of tin.

❺ Roll out 250 g (8 oz) of marzipan and cut out an 18 cm (7 inch) circle. Place this over mixture in tin and cover it with remaining fruit mixture.

❻ Bake cake in a preheated oven at 150 °C (300 °F/gas 2) for 2 hours, until lightly browned.

❼ Allow to cool in tin. Wrap in cling film so that it is airtight, and store for at least a week.

❽ When ready to use, brush surface of cake with apricot jam and cover with a circle of marzipan. Crimp edges of marzipan and brush again with jam. Make marzipan balls and position them on surface.

❾ Grill a few minutes until browned. Decorate with fruit and ribbon if desired. Keep in an airtight container for up to 2 weeks.

TIP

Watch cake constantly while it is under the grill and turn it around when necessary. This will ensure even browning of the marzipan and prevent it from burning.

EASTER BISCUITS

280 g (9 oz) plain flour
pinch ground mixed spice
pinch ground cinnamon
125 g (4 oz) butter
125 g (4 oz) caster sugar
45 g (1½ oz) currants
2.5 ml (½ tsp) lemon rind
1 egg, beaten
about 30 ml (2 tbsp) milk
caster sugar

❶ Sift dry ingredients together. Rub in butter until mixture resembles fine breadcrumbs.

❷ Add remaining ingredients except caster sugar and mix to a stiff dough.

❸ Roll out to a thickness of 3 mm (⅛ inch). Cut rounds with a biscuit cutter and place on a lightly greased baking tray.

❹ Bake in a preheated oven at 180 °C (350 °F/gas 4) for 15 minutes. Sprinkle with caster sugar.

❺ Cool on a wire rack and store in an airtight container.

Makes about 45

TIP

For a crisper biscuit, substitute lard for half the butter.

NUTTY EASTER TREAT

DOUGH
560 g (1 lb 2 oz) white bread flour
125 g (4 oz) caster sugar
2.5 ml (½ tsp) salt
10 g (⅓ oz) instant dry yeast
200 ml (6½ fl oz) lukewarm milk
90 g (3 oz) butter or margarine, melted
2 eggs, beaten

FILLING
60 g (2 oz) walnuts, coarsely chopped
30 g (1 oz) pecan nuts, coarsely chopped
45 g (1½ oz) almonds, coarsely chopped
60 g (2 oz) butter or margarine, melted
30 ml (2 tbsp) honey or golden syrup
15 ml (1 tbsp) ground cinnamon

TOPPING
Glacé Icing (page 67)
glazed fruit

❶ Sift flour, sugar and salt together. Add yeast.

❷ Add milk to dry ingredients with melted butter and eggs, to form a soft dough. Knead for 10 minutes, until smooth and elastic.

❸ Place dough in a greased plastic bag and allow to rise for about 30 minutes, until double in size.

❹ For filling: Mix nuts with remaining filling ingredients.

❺ Knock down the dough and allow to rise for a further 10 minutes.

❻ Flatten dough into a 45 x 30 cm (18 x 12 inch) rectangle. Spread with filling. Roll up from the long side.

❼ Join the two ends of the roll together to form a circle. Using a pair of scissors, make 20 cuts into the circle, each three-quarters of the width of the dough. Turn each wedge on its side.

❽ Place on a greased baking tray and bake at 180 °C (350 °F/gas 4) for 35 minutes, until golden brown.

❾ Pour the Glacé Icing over the warm ring and decorate with glazed fruit.

From top: Nutty Easter Treat, Simnel Cake and Easter Biscuits.

FRUIT CAKES

Rich fruit cakes should be made at least two months before Christmas to develop the flavours.

Lining the tin

To ensure a well-shaped cake, it is most important to line the cake tin correctly. Lining the tin protects the cake during the long cooking process, so the longer the cooking time, the heavier the lining should be. For a 20 cm (8 inch) square cake tin two layers of brown paper or two layers of greaseproof paper should be used. If baking for longer than 3 hours, the lining paper should stand a few centimetres (inches) above the edge of the tin to protect the top of the cake.

First cut the strips for the sides of the tin, then use the base of the tin as a guide for cutting the paper.

Preparing cake mixture

Eggs and butter should be at room temperature. Add sugar until just combined. Add eggs one at a time and do not overmix. Add fruit mixture to creamed mixture and mix ingredients well (rich fruit cakes do not contain any raising agent). Spoon mixture carefully into the lined tin and level top with a spatula.

When baking more than one cake at a time, the cooking time will be a little longer due to greater absorption of heat.

After removing the cake from the oven, leave it in the tin to cool completely. Then brush it with brandy to soften the surface.

Remove cake from tin, sprinkle more brandy over, and store in an airtight container for up to six months or in the refrigerator or freezer for one year. Sprinkle a little brandy over the cake once a month to keep it moist.

MOIST CHRISTMAS CAKE

725 g (1½ lb) mixed dried fruit
125 g (4 oz) stoned dates, finely chopped
210 g (7 oz) glacé cherries, halved
60 g (2 oz) pecan nuts or walnuts, chopped
125 ml (4 fl oz) brandy
250 g (8 oz) butter
180 g (6 oz) brown sugar
5 eggs
15 ml (1 tbsp) sieved apricot jam
280 g (9 oz) plain flour
pinch salt
2.5 ml (½ tsp) ground nutmeg
2.5 ml (½ tsp) ground cinnamon
5 ml (1 tsp) mixed spice
5 ml (1 tsp) ground ginger
2.5 ml (½ tsp) ground cloves
2.5 ml (½ tsp) bicarbonate of soda

ICING
marzipan
ready-to-roll icing

❶ Mix dried fruit, dates, cherries, nuts and brandy together and leave overnight.

❷ Cream butter and sugar together and add eggs; beat well after each addition until light and fluffy. Add jam and fruit mixture, mixing well.

❸ Add sifted dry ingredients and mix well.

❹ Line a 20 cm (8 inch) square cake tin with two layers brown paper or two layers greaseproof paper. Grease well, turn mixture into tin and level top of cake mixture with spatula. Bake in a preheated oven at 150 °C (300 °F/ gas 2) for 2¼ hours.

❺ Test centre of cake with a skewer. If baked, skewer will come out clean.

❻ Allow to cool completely in tin. Turn out and remove lining. Sprinkle with brandy; seal with cling film.

❼ Store in a cool place. Sprinkle brandy over cake once a month.

❽ Spread thin layer of jam over entire cake. Cover with marzipan and ice with ready-to-roll icing or Royal Icing (page 67).

BOILED FRUIT CAKE

500 g (1 lb) mixed dried fruit
110 g (3½ oz) glacé cherries, halved
250 g (8 oz) sugar
90 g (3 oz) butter or margarine
250 ml (8 fl oz) water
280 g (9 oz) plain flour
10 ml (2 tsp) bicarbonate of soda
2.5 ml (½ tsp) salt
1 egg, beaten
60 ml (4 tbsp) brandy

❶ Boil dried fruit, cherries, sugar, butter and water together for about 10 minutes. Leave to cool.

❷ Sift the flour, bicarbonate of soda and salt together and stir well into the fruit mixture.

❸ Mix in beaten egg and brandy. Line a 20 cm (8 inch) round, loose-bottomed cake tin with one layer brown paper or three layers greaseproof paper. Grease well and turn mixture into tin.

❹ Bake in a preheated oven at 150 °C (300 °F/gas 2) for 1¼ hours. Test centre of cake with a skewer. If baked, skewer will come out clean. Leave in turned-off oven for a while to prevent sinking. Remove from oven.

❺ Allow to cool completely in tin before turning out. Sprinkle with brandy and seal. Allow to mature for at least 2 weeks.

VARIATIONS

If you run out of brandy or do not wish to use it, substitute pure apricot juice. It preserves just as well.

For individual fruit cakes: Turn mixture into three x 12 cm (5 inch) round ovenproof bowls and bake in a preheated oven at 150 °C (300 °F/gas 2) for 45 minutes.

TIP

If the top of your fruit cake is a little too crusty for your taste, cover it with a layer of sliced raw apple. Leave in an airtight container for 24 hours. After a day the crust will become soft and moist and the apple slices can be removed.

Clockwise from top: Christmas Tree Biscuits, Boiled Fruit Cake and Moist Christmas Cake.

CHRISTMAS TREE BISCUITS

125 g (4 oz) margarine
125 g (4 oz) caster sugar
5 ml (1 tsp) vanilla extract
1 egg
280 g (9 oz) plain flour
60 ml (4 tbsp) cornflour
5 ml (1 tsp) baking powder
2.5 ml (½ tsp) salt
Glacé Icing (page 67)

❶ Beat margarine and sugar together.

Add extract and egg and beat until light and fluffy.

❷ Sift dry ingredients, add to creamed mixture and knead to form a stiff dough.

❸ Roll out to a thickness of 3 mm (⅛ inch) and, using a Christmas biscuit cutter, cut into shapes. For hanging the biscuits from a tree, make a hole in the dough.

❹ Place on a greased baking tray and bake in a preheated oven at 180 °C (350 °F/gas 4) for 10–15 minutes, or until light brown on the edges.

❺ Remove biscuits from tray using a spatula; place on a wire rack to cool.

❺ Ice with Glacé Icing and decorate with silver balls, and so on. Christmas biscuits may also be dipped into melted chocolate before decorating.

Makes about 40

TIP

For hanging biscuits, make a hole for the ribbon with an icing nozzle

---

STEAMED PUDDINGS

Steamed sponge puddings, traditionally eaten at Christmas time, have a finer texture than baked sponge cakes. They are usually steamed in a cloth, but are equally good steamed in a metal bowl.

Preparing the bowl

Grease the inside of the bowl and line the base with greaseproof paper. Place a topping such as fruit on the bottom and fill the bowl to about 5 cm (2 inches) from the top. Cover with greaseproof paper, then seal with metal lid to prevent water from entering. Place the bowl on a wire rack in a saucepan so that it does not touch the bottom of the pan. This will ensure even cooking.

Steaming and reheating

Christmas puddings are steamed for at least 2 hours and can be kept, sealed, for 2–3 months. Reheat by steaming over a saucepan for 30 minutes or heat in a preheated oven at 180 °C (350 °F/gas 4) for 30 minutes.

TRADITIONAL CHRISTMAS PUDDING

180 g (6 oz) raisins
250 ml (8 fl oz) brandy or sherry
250 g (8 oz) butter
250 g (8 oz) sugar
4 eggs
150 g (5 oz) plain flour
10 ml (2 tsp) bicarbonate of soda
2.5 ml (½ tsp) salt
10 ml (2 tsp) ground cinnamon
2.5 ml (½ tsp) ground ginger
2.5 ml (½ tsp) ground nutmeg
2.5 ml (½ tsp) allspice
150 g (5 oz) stoned dates, chopped
150 g (5 oz) currants
125 g (4 oz)d pecan nuts, chopped
125 g (4 oz) raw carrot, finely grated
60 g (2 oz) fresh breadcrumbs
45 ml (3 tbsp) golden syrup
15 ml (1 tbsp) grated lemon rind
15 ml (1 tbsp) grated orange rind

❶ Soak raisins in brandy or sherry overnight.

❷ Beat butter and sugar together. Add eggs, one at a time, beating well after each addition.

❸ Sift dry ingredients together, add to creamed mixture, and mix well. Add remaining ingredients and raisins.

❹ Spoon mixture into a greased 2 litre (3 pints) metal pudding bowl. Cover with a double layer of foil or greaseproof paper and secure with string or a metal top.

❺ Place on a wire rack in a large saucepan and pour in boiling water, to reach halfway up sides of bowl.

❻ Steam for 2½–3 hours, or until well cooked, remembering to check water level and refill if necessary.

❼ Allow to stand in bowl for at least 20 minutes before turning out.

❽ Serve hot with brandy sauce or cream.

Serves 8-10

TIPS

To reheat, steam pudding for 30 minutes as directed in the recipe.

Place a tea towel over the top of the bowl before placing the lid on the saucepan, as this absorbs the condensation and prevents the pudding from going soggy.

To form a handle: Cover bowl with layers of greaseproof paper and tie with string just below the rim. Also form a loop above the bowl. This will serve as a useful handle.

Brandy Sauce

30 g (1 oz) butter
250 g (8 oz) caster sugar
45 ml (3 tbsp) brandy
2 eggs, separated
125 ml (4 fl oz) single cream or milk

❶ Using a double boiler, melt butter while gradually beating in sugar.

❷ Add brandy, beat well, add egg yolks, and cream.

❸ Cook until thickened.

❹ Beat egg whites and fold in lightly until smooth. Serve hot.

MINCEPIES

These pies were originally made in an oval shape to symbolize Christ's crib.

1 quantity Cream Cheese Pastry (page 31) OR 1 quantity Rich Shortcrust Pastry (page 31)
440 g (14 oz) jar fruit mincemeat
1 egg white
caster sugar

❶ Roll out pastry to a thickness of 3 mm (⅛ inch). Cut out rounds to fit base of patty pan tins or bun tins. Cut the same number of smaller circles to form the lids of mincepies.

❷ Place 5 ml (1 tsp) fruit mincemeat on the base of each pastry round.

❸ Dampen pastry edge with water, cover with pastry lid, and seal. Prick holes in the lid with a fork or make a small incision with the tip of a sharp knife. Brush with lightly beaten egg white or iced water.

❹ Bake in a preheated oven at 200 ºC (400 °F/gas 6) for 15 minutes, or until golden brown. Sprinkle with caster sugar while still warm.

Makes 16

TIPS

Place a small piece of unsalted butter in fruit pies to prevent juice from running out when baking.

Fruit mincepies freeze well.

Clockwise from top right: Traditional Christmas Pudding, Christmas Mincemeat Slices and Mincepies.

CHRISTMAS MINCEMEAT SLICES

125 g (4 oz) margarine
45 ml (3 tbsp) caster sugar
25 ml (5 tsp) oil
1 egg
5 ml (1 tsp) vanilla extract
280 g (9 oz) plain flour
10 ml (2 tsp) baking powder
pinch salt
440 g (14 oz) jar fruit mincemeat
1 apple, peeled and grated
25 ml (5 tbsp) brandy
icing sugar for dusting

❶ Cream margarine and sugar well.

❷ Add oil, egg and extract, and beat well together.

❸ Sift dry ingredients together and knead into creamed mixture to form a dough.

❹ Press half of dough into a greased 23 cm (9 inch) round ovenproof dish or 23 cm (9 inch) square cake tin.

❺ Mix fruit mincemeat, apple and brandy together and spread thickly over dough.

❻ Coarsely grate remaining dough over mincemeat.

❼ Bake in a preheated oven at 180 °C (350 °F/gas 4) for 20 minutes, or until golden brown.

❽ Dust with icing sugar before slicing.

VARIATION

Substitute apricot jam or lemon curd for mincemeat and grated apple.

TIP

The pastry can be kept, wrapped, in the refrigerator for 2 days.

11

TRADITIONAL RECIPES

MANY OF THE DISHES WE ENJOY TODAY HAVE BEEN INHERITED OVER THE CENTURIES FROM THE DUTCH, THE MALAYSIANS AND THE FRENCH HUGUENOTS – AND FAVOURITE RECIPES, OFTEN CHARACTERISTIC OF A PARTICULAR REGION – HAVE BEEN PASSED DOWN FROM ONE GENERATION TO THE NEXT. THIS CHAPTER CONTAINS A SELECTION OF TRADITIONAL SWEET TREATS, SOME OF WHICH MAY BE UNFAMILIAR.

MILK TART

The milk tart, with its puff pastry base borrowed from the French, was introduced to South Africa by the Dutch.

BASE
60 g (2 oz) butter
30 ml (2 tbsp) sugar
1 egg
110 g (3½ oz) self-raising flour
pinch of salt
15 ml (1 tbsp) milk

FILLING
500 ml (16 fl oz) milk
75 ml (5 tbsp) sugar
90 g (3 oz) plain flour
2 eggs, separated
pinch of salt
30 g (1 oz) butter
5 ml (1 tsp) vanilla extract
ground cinnamon

❶ For base: Beat butter and sugar together. Add egg and beat until light and fluffy. Sift flour and salt together; add, with milk, to creamed mixture.

❷ Grease a 23 cm (9 inch) ovenproof flan dish and press the dough into it using a spatula.

❸ For filling: Heat milk and sugar together in a heavy-based saucepan.

❹ Add some of the warm milk to flour and return to saucepan. Add egg yolks and salt.

❺ Boil until thickened, stirring frequently. Remove from heat, add butter and vanilla extract, and fold in lightly beaten egg whites.

❻ Pour into base, sprinkle with cinnamon, and bake in a preheated oven at 180 °C (350 °F/gas 4) for 30 minutes.

TIP

Do not overbeat egg whites.

HERTZOG COOKIES

280 g (9 oz) plain flour
10 ml (2 tsp) baking powder
pinch of salt
45 ml (3 tbsp) caster sugar
125 g (4 oz) margarine
3 large eggs, separated
45 ml (3 tbsp) water
200 g (6½ oz) sieved apricot jam
315 g (10 oz) sugar
180 g (6 oz) desiccated coconut

❶ Sift the flour, baking powder and salt together. Add caster sugar and rub in margarine.

❷ Beat egg yolks and water together and add to dry ingredients, mixing to form a soft dough.

❸ Roll dough out thinly and press out circles. Line the base of greased patty pan tins with dough circles.

❹ Spoon a teaspoonful of apricot jam on to middle of each circle of dough.

❺ Beat egg whites until soft peak stage. Add sugar gradually, while still beating. Add coconut and spoon egg mixture on to apricot jam filling.

❻ Bake in a preheated oven at 180 °C (350 °F/gas 4) for 20–25 minutes. Turn on to a wire rack to cool.

Makes 25–30

TIP

When making jam tarts, put spoonfuls of apricot jam into a plastic bag containing flour. Shake the bag until the jam is well coated with flour, then place on pastry. This will ensure that the jam does not 'leak' during baking.

CINNAMON DUMPLINGS

140 g (4½ oz) plain flour
10 ml (2 tsp) baking powder
2.5 ml (½ oz) salt
45 g (1½ oz) margarine or butter
1 egg
90 ml (6 tbsp) milk
500 ml (16 fl oz) boiling water
30 g (1 oz) margarine or butter
cinnamon sugar

❶ Sift the dry ingredients together. Rub in 45 g (1½ oz) margarine or butter until mixture resembles breadcrumbs.

❷ Beat egg and milk together, stir into flour, and mix to a soft dough. Add extra milk if necessary.

❸ Bring water and 30 g (1 oz) margarine or butter to boil. Place spoonfuls of dough in boiling water. Cover with lid and allow to boil for 15 minutes. Do not remove lid while cooking.

❹ Remove dumplings with a slotted spoon and place in a serving dish. Sprinkle with cinnamon sugar.

❺ Bring water in which dumplings were cooked to the boil again. Add more cinnamon sugar and pour over dumplings. More water can be added if necessary.

Serves 4

TIP

Before rubbing into flour, chill butter or margarine until very hard, and grate coarsely. This will save time and result in a light texture.

Clockwise from top: Hertzog Cookies, Cinnamon Dumplings and Milk Tart.

SPICE COOKIES

Originally, spice cookies were decorated with 'rooi bolus' – a red powder mixed with the dough.

470 g (15 oz) plain flour
5 ml (1 tsp) salt
5 ml (1 tsp) ground cloves
5 ml (1 tsp) ground mixed spice
5 ml (1 tsp) ground cinnamon
5 ml (1 tsp) bicarbonate of soda
250 g (8 oz) sugar
125 g (4 oz) butter
125 g (4 oz) lard
2 eggs, beaten
125 ml (4 fl oz) sweet red wine

❶ Sift dry ingredients together and add sugar.

❷ Rub in butter and lard until mixture resembles breadcrumbs.

❸ Add beaten eggs and red wine and mix to a soft dough.

❹ Leave to stand a few hours, or overnight if possible.

❺ Roll out to a thickness of 3 mm (⅛ inch) and cut out cookies with a biscuit cutter.

❻ Place on a greased baking tray and bake in a preheated oven at 200 ˚C (400 ˚F/gas 6) for 10–12 minutes.

Makes about 80, depending on size

MUST BUNS

These buns originated in the Cape winelands in South Africa, where they were made from dough leavened with must – the juice of the grape in the first stages of fermentation – instead of yeast. If fresh grapes were not available, raisins were used instead.

340 g (11 oz) unseeded raisins
about 375 ml (¾ pint) lukewarm water
2.5 kg (5½ lb) plain flour
280 ml (9 fl oz) warm milk
250 g (8 oz) butter
15 ml (1 tbsp) salt
400 g (13 oz) sugar
30 ml (2 tbsp) whole aniseed

❶ Chop raisins in food processor. Add lukewarm water and leave, covered, to ferment for four days. When raisins have risen to the surface, the yeast – or must – is ready.

❷ Strain yeast through a muslin cloth and reserve liquid to make yeast mixture rise. Discard raisins.

❸ Prepare yeast sponge mixture by adding 150 g (5 oz) of the flour to liquid and mixing to a thin batter. Beat slightly, cover, and leave in a warm place until double in size.

❹ Add warm milk to butter and allow to stand.

❺ Sift the remaining flour and salt together. Add sugar, butter mixture, yeast mixture and aniseed, mixing well. Add more milk if necessary.

❻ Brush surface of dough with melted butter, cover, and leave to rise in a warm place overnight.

❼ Knock down, cover, and again leave to rise in a warm place until dough has doubled in size.

❽ Shape dough into balls and pack tightly in greased deep loaf tins. Brush with melted butter. Leave in a warm place to rise until double in size.

❾ Bake in a preheated oven at 180 ˚C (350 ˚F/gas 4) for about 1 hour, until golden brown.

Makes about 160 buns
depending on size

> **TIP**
>
> *A mixer with a dough hook is ideal for making these buns.*

MILK NOODLES

A traditional dish with a lumpy texture that is cooked with milk and flour and served with cinnamon sugar as a light meal.

2 litres (3½ pints) milk
165 g (5½ oz) plain flour
5 ml (1 tsp) salt
15 g (½ oz) margarine or butter
cinnamon sugar

❶ Bring milk to the boil.

❷ Sift the flour and salt together and rub in margarine. Add to milk and beat. Lumps will form, but keep stirring well.

❸ Cover with lid and simmer for 5–8 minutes, until cooked.

❹ Serve hot with cinnamon sugar.

Serves 4

DEEP-FRIED DOUGH CAKES

280 g (9 oz) self-raising flour
2.5 ml (½ tsp) salt
25 ml (5 tsp) sugar
1 egg, beaten
about 280 ml (9 fl oz) milk or water
cooking oil for deep-frying

❶ Sift flour and salt together and add sugar.

❷ Mix egg and water together and stir into dry ingredients. Mix until a sticky dough is formed.

❸ Deep-fry spoonfuls of dough in hot oil until golden brown on both sides. Drain on paper towels.

❹ Serve with butter and syrup, honey or preserves.

Makes 20

> **TIP**
>
> *The dough cakes should preferably be eaten on the same day as cooked.*

Clockwise from top: Must Buns, Milk Noodles, Spice Cookies and Deep-Fried Dough Cakes.

SYRUP PLAITS

SYRUP
1.2 kg (2 lb 6 oz) sugar
750 ml (1¼ pints) water
2.5 ml (½ tsp) cream of tartar
5 ml (1 tsp) cold water
2.5 ml (½ tsp) ground ginger
1 cinnamon stick
OR
pinch ground cinnamon
rind of 1 lemon
20 ml (4 tsp) lemon juice

DOUGH
560 g (1 lb 2 oz) plain flour
20 ml (4 tsp) baking powder
5 ml (1 tsp) salt
30 g (1 oz) margarine
15 ml (1 tbsp) sugar
2 eggs
about 250 ml (8 fl oz) water
cooking oil for frying

❶ For syrup: In a large saucepan, dissolve the sugar in the water and bring to the boil.

❷ Mix cream of tartar and cold water together and add to the syrup. Add ginger, cinnamon, lemon rind and lemon juice.

❸ Boil for 10 minutes and leave to cool. Refrigerate until very cold – overnight, if possible.

❹ For dough: Sift dry ingredients together. Rub in margarine until the mixture resembles fine breadcrumbs. Add sugar.

❺ Beat eggs with 200 ml (6½ fl oz) water and add to dry ingredients, mixing to a soft dough. Add more water if necessary.

❻ Knead the dough lightly for a few minutes, until smooth. Cover with cling film and leave to rest for at least 1 hour.

❼ Roll out dough to a thickness of 5 mm (¼ inch). Cut strips 1 cm (½ inch) wide and 7.5 cm (3 inches) long. Join ends of 3 strips and plait. Alternatively, take two strips 15 cm (6 inches) long, join ends and roll.

❽ Deep-fry plaits in oil until brown on both sides. Dip immediately into ice cold syrup, making sure that the plaits are soaked through.

❾ Remove with a slotted spoon and turn on to a wire rack. If syrup becomes warm, return to the refrigerator. Store plaits in the refrigerator before serving.

Makes 48

TIPS

Do not fry plaits too quickly or the outside will be cooked, and the inside still raw.

Use two bowls of syrup. Keep one in the refrigerator while using the other.

Keep plaits in the freezer and remove 30 minutes before use.

BROWN PUDDING

1 egg
125 g (4 oz) sugar
15 ml (1 tbsp) sieved apricot jam
150 g (5 oz) plain flour
5 ml (1 tsp) baking powder
5 ml (1 tsp) bicarbonate of soda
pinch of salt
20 ml (4 tsp) vinegar
250 ml (8 fl oz) milk

SYRUP
250 g (8 oz) sugar
250 ml (8 fl oz) milk
125 ml (4 fl oz) boiling water
45 g (1½ oz) butter
5 ml (1 tsp) vanilla extract

❶ Beat egg and sugar together until light and fluffy.

❷ Add remaining ingredients, except milk, beating well. Beat in milk and pour mixture into a greased, medium-sized ovenproof dish. Bake in a preheated oven at 180 °C (350 °F/gas 4) for 40–50 minutes.

❸ For syrup: Boil all ingredients except extract in a saucepan for 5 minutes. Add extract.

❹ Spoon syrup over hot pudding.

Serves 4-6

TIPSY TART

60 g (2 oz) margarine
200 g (6½ oz) sugar
250 g (8 oz) stoned dates, chopped
375 ml (12 fl oz) boiling water
5 ml (1 tsp) bicarbonate of soda
2 eggs
210 g (7 oz) plain flour
5 ml (1 tsp) baking powder
2.5 ml (½ tsp) salt
60 g (2 oz) walnuts, chopped

SYRUP
250 g (8 oz) sugar
125 ml (4 fl oz) water
60 g (2 oz) margarine
5 ml (1 tsp) vanilla extract
75 ml (5 tbsp) brandy

❶ Mix margarine, sugar, dates and boiling water with bicarbonate of soda in a mixing bowl and leave to cool. Beat eggs and add to mixture.

❷ Sift flour, baking powder and salt together and add, with walnuts, to date mixture. Mix well.

❸ Spoon into a greased ovenproof dish and bake in a preheated oven at 180 °C (350 °F/gas 4) for 30 minutes.

❹ For syrup: Boil sugar, water and margarine together for 15 minutes. Add extract and brandy.

❺ Remove tart from oven; pour syrup over. Serve with cream or custard.

Clockwise from top right: Tipsy Tart, Pumpkin Fritters and Syrup Plaits.

PUMPKIN FRITTERS

440 g (14 oz) cooked, mashed pumpkin
75 g (2½ oz) plain flour
5 ml (1 tsp) baking powder
2.5 ml (½ tsp) salt
2 eggs, beaten
about 30 ml (2 tbsp) milk
cinnamon sugar
cooking oil for frying

❶ Mix pumpkin, flour, baking powder and salt together.

❷ Add eggs and enough milk to form a batter.

❸ Shallow-fry spoonfuls of mixture in hot oil on both sides, until brown.

❹ Drain on paper towels and sprinkle with cinnamon sugar.

Makes 18, depending on size

> ### TIP
>
> *To make cinnamon sugar, mix 90 g (3 oz) caster sugar with 10 ml (2 tsp) ground cinnamon.*

117

12

BAKING FOR CHILDREN

MOST CHILDREN REACH A STAGE WHEN THEY WANT TO GET INVOLVED IN BAKING. THE RECIPES INCLUDED IN THE FIRST SECTION OF THIS CHAPTER ARE IDEAL FOR CHILDREN TO MAKE BY THEMSELVES, WITH A LITTLE SUPERVISION IF NECESSARY, OR EVEN FOR YOU TO PUT TOGETHER QUICKLY.
BIRTHDAY CAKES, COVERED IN THE SECOND SECTION, ARE ALWAYS THE HIGHLIGHT OF THE PARTY AND NEEDN'T BE TIME-CONSUMING OR DIFFICULT TO MAKE. WITH A LITTLE IMAGINATION, A BASIC SPONGE CAN BE TURNED INTO SOMETHING SPECIAL — AND THE BIRTHDAY GIRL OR BOY WILL ENJOY HELPING WITH THE DECORATING.

TIP

Cutters with different shapes and sizes are available from kitchen shops. If unable to get a suitable one, draw your own shape of a man or a woman on a piece of stiff cardboard and cut out. Place shape on rolled-out dough and cut around it with a sharp knife.

For the small baker

CUP CAKES

125 g (4 oz) margarine
200 g (6½ oz) caster sugar
5 ml (1 tsp) vanilla extract
2 eggs
280 g (9 oz) self-raising flour
2.5 ml (½ tsp) salt
200 ml (6½ fl oz) milk
whipping cream
caster sugar
icing sugar

❶ Place 24 paper cake cases on a baking sheet or in muffin tins.

❷ Cream margarine and sugar until smooth and creamy. Add extract and eggs, beating well after each addition. Fold in sifted flour and salt alternately with milk.

❸ Spoon into paper cases until three-quarters full. Bake in a preheated oven at 200 °C (400 °F/gas 6) for 12-15 minutes.

❹ To make butterfly cakes, cut a thin slice from the top of each cup cake, and cut slice in half down centre. Whip cream stiffly with a little caster sugar. Place cream on top of each cake.

❺ Place cut tops on cream to resemble wings, and dust with icing sugar.

Makes 24

VARIATION

ORANGE CUP CAKES

Add 5 ml (1 tsp) orange extract and 10 ml (2 tsp) grated orange rind to mixture.

TIP

Ice cakes with Glacé Icing (page 67).

GINGERBREAD MEN

125 g (4 oz) butter
90 g (3 oz) soft brown sugar
1 egg yolk
280 g (9 oz) plain flour
5 ml (1 tsp) bicarbonate of soda
10 ml (2 tsp) ground ginger
5 ml (1 tsp) ground cinnamon
45 ml (3 tbsp) golden syrup
about 45 ml (3 tbsp) water

ROYAL ICING
1 egg white
280 g (9 oz) icing sugar
food colouring

❶ Cream butter and sugar until light and fluffy. Add egg yolk and beat well.

❷ Sift dry ingredients together and add, with syrup and enough water, to make a stiff dough. Roll dough to a thickness of about 5 mm (¼ inch) and cut gingerbread figures with a special cutter.

❸ Place on greased trays and bake in a preheated oven at 180 °C (350 °F/gas 4) for 10 minutes. Turn on to a wire rack to cool.

❹ For icing: Lightly beat egg white. Gradually add sifted icing sugar, beating well. Beat to piping con-sistency and add food colouring of choice. Pipe detail on gingerbread figures.

Makes 12, depending on size of cutter

VARIATION

Royal icing can be replaced with raisins or chocolate chips for the eyes and buttons. Cut strips of cherry for the mouth.

CHOCOLATE CHIP CRUNCHIES

250 g (8 oz) butter or margarine
250 g (8 oz) sugar
150 g (5 oz) brown bread flour
2.5 ml (½ tsp) salt
180 g (6 oz) rolled oats
90 g (3 oz) desiccated coconut
150 g (5 oz) chocolate chips
30 ml (2 tbsp) golden syrup
5 ml (1 tsp) vanilla extract
2.5 ml (½ tsp) bicarbonate of soda
45 ml (3 tbsp) boiling water

❶ Cream butter and sugar together.

❷ Sift brown bread flour and salt and add bran left behind in sieve.

❸ Add to creamed mixture with oats, coconut, chocolate chips, syrup and extract.

❹ Dissolve bicarbonate of soda in water and add, mixing well.

❺ Place teaspoonfuls of mixture on a greased baking tray and flatten with a spoon. Leave enough space for spreading during baking.

❻ Bake in a preheated oven at 180 °C (350 °F/gas 4) for 15 minutes.

Makes about 50

VARIATIONS

Substitute raisins for chocolate.

Substitute rice crispies for oats.

Clockwise from top left: Chocolate Chip Crunchies, Jam Slices, Cup Cakes, Butterfly Cakes and Gingerbread Men.

JAM SLICES

125 g (4 oz) margarine
125 g (4 oz) sugar
1 egg
5 ml (1 tsp) vanilla extract
280 g (9 oz) plain flour
10 ml (2 tsp) baking powder
about 165 g (5½ oz) sieved apricot jam
icing sugar

❶ Beat margarine and sugar well.

❷ Add egg and extract and beat until light and fluffy. Add sifted dry ingredients and knead well.

❸ Press half the dough into a greased 20 x 25 cm (8 x 10 inch) rectangular baking tin. Spread a layer of jam over dough.

❹ Coarsely grate remaining dough over jam.

❺ Bake in a preheated oven at 180 °C (350 °F/gas 4) for 20 minutes, or until golden brown. Leave for a few minutes to cool. Cut into squares and leave to cool in pan. Dust with icing sugar.

Makes 20, depending on size

PLAY DOUGH

280 g (9 oz) plain flour
500 ml (16 fl oz) water
125 g (4 oz) table salt
15 ml (1 tbsp) cream of tartar
15 ml (1 tbsp) cooking oil
5 ml (1 tsp) food colouring of choice

❶ Mix together all ingredients except food colouring in a heavy-based saucepan. Stir over medium heat until mixture forms a ball in the middle.

❷ Leave to cool and knead well. Add colouring and knead again.

❸ Keep in an airtight container or plastic bag to prevent drying out.

TIPS

Dip a skewer into food colouring and shake drops from skewer onto dough to achieve desired colour.

Return dough to the plastic bag or airtight container to ensure that it lasts longer and does not dry out.

Birthday cakes

Serve birthday cakes on a cake board covered with paper or foil, and decorated with desiccated coconut, sweets, popcorn, hundreds-and-thousands, or flakes.

TREASURE CHEST

2 x Chocolate Oil Cake (page 50)
sieved apricot jam
Chocolate Icing (page 66)
chocolate coins
costume jewellery
sweets

❶ Follow basic recipe for chocolate cake, using two 23 cm (9 inch) loaf tins. For layer 1, fill one-third full and bake 20 minutes. For layer 2, fill two-thirds full and bake 40–45 minutes.

❷ Assemble using icing as shown in illustration. Ice cake and decorate as shown in photograph.

HANSEL AND GRETEL

2 x Hot Milk Sponge Cake (page 57)
sieved apricot jam
Basic Icing (page 66)
food colouring of choice
liquorice strips
Smarties
wafer biscuits
4 chocolate flakes
desiccated coconut

❶ Follow basic recipe for sponge cake, but bake in two 23 cm loaf tins for 50–55 minutes.

❷ Cut cooled cake and assemble using apricot jam, as shown in illustrations. Ice cake and decorate as shown in photograph.

TIP

To colour desiccated coconut: Sprinkle on a tray and mix in a few drops of desired colouring. Leave to dry.

Layer 1

Trim layer 1 to form the lid and attach to layer 2 with icing

Layer 2

Trim one of the loaves to form the roof, then attach the roof to the house using apricot jam

Treasure Chest Cake.

Hansel and Gretel Cake.

MICKEY MOUSE CAKE

**2 x 20 cm (8 inch) Hot Milk Sponge
Cake layers (page 57)
sieved apricot jam
½ quantity Basic Icing (page 66)
½ quantity Chocolate Icing (page 66)
chocolate rounds
chocolate vermicelli
liquorice strips
fruit drop for mouth**

❶ Follow basic recipe for sponge cake.

❷ Cut cooled cake and assemble using
apricot jam, as shown in illustrations.

❸ Ice cake and decorate as shown in
photograph.

TIP

*For a darker icing, substitute butter
in icing with white margarine.*

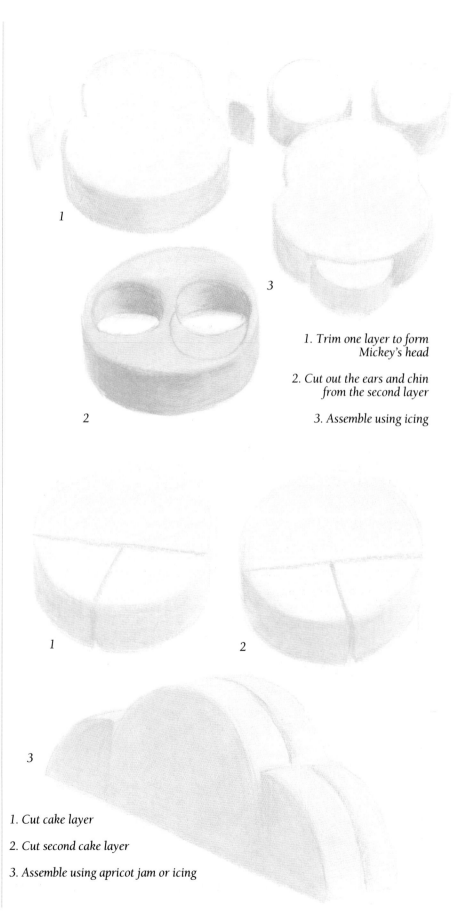

1. *Trim one layer to form
Mickey's head*

2. *Cut out the ears and chin
from the second layer*

3. *Assemble using icing*

DINOSAUR

**2 x 20 cm (8 inch) Chocolate Oil Cake
layers (page 50)
sieved apricot jam
Chocolate Icing (page 66)
wafer biscuits
flat round chocolates
Smarties
chocolate sticks
liquorice strips
hundreds-and-thousands
desiccated coconut**

❶ Cut cooled cake and assemble
using apricot jam or icing, as shown
in illustrations.

❷ Ice cake and decorate as shown in
photograph.

TIP

*To make round flat chocolates: Melt
plain cooking chocolate over
saucepan of boiling water, stirring
occasionally. Spread smoothly on to
greaseproof paper. Allow to set and
cut out rounds.*

---

1. *Cut cake layer*

2. *Cut second cake layer*

3. *Assemble using apricot jam or icing*

Mickey Mouse Cake.

Dinosaur Cake.

DEALING WITH FLOPS

Unfortunately, flops are a reality that even the best cook has to face! However, a flop needn't be the end of the world, and, with a little patience and imagination, can probably be salvaged.

Here we give you a few ideas as to what to do with cakes that don't meet your expectations. Some are suitable for cakes that have fallen apart; others for cakes that haven't risen.

Make petits fours

Cut the cake into 3 x 3 cm (1¼ x 1¼ inches) squares and sandwich pairs of squares together with jam. Follow instructions given for Petits Fours (page 58).

Make a gâteau

Cut the cake horizontally into four layers. Pour 15 ml (1 tbsp) sherry on to layers. Spread two of the layers with confectioner's custard (page 43) and the remaining two with whipped cream. Assemble the cake, starting with a custard layer and ending with a cream layer. Decorate the cake with cream, grated chocolate and other appropriate decorations.

Make a ring cake

If the cake has sunk in the centre, cut out the centre and make a ring cake. Fill with fresh fruit, then ice and decorate.

Make lamingtons

Cut the cake into large squares. Follow the recipe given for Lamingtons (page 60).

Make a trifle

Use large squares of sponge cake and follow the recipe given for trifle (page 102).

Use smaller offcuts from cakes for making crumbs and use them as you would breadcrumbs, or bake them in the oven until golden brown and serve with cream or custard. Smaller crumbs can be used for making truffles or in steamed puddings.

CAKE FLAWS

FLAW	REASON FOR FLAW
Cake rises to a point	Over-manipulation
	Batter too stiff
	Initial oven temperature too high
Surface of cake not level	Uneven heat penetration (tins touch each other or oven sides)
	Oven not level
Cake sinks in middle	Too much sugar used
	Batter too dry
	Under-manipulation
	Tin too small
	Oven temperature too low
	Cake moved during baking
	Cake not cooked
	Oven door opened during baking
	Too much raising agent used
Cake does not rise	Tins too large
	Inactive raising agent
	Ingredients too cold
Mixture runs over the top	Tins too small
	Too much raising agent used
	Too much sugar used
Cake rises and sinks while in oven	Too much liquid used
	Too much raising agent used
	Oven door opened too soon/too frequently
Cake sticks to baking tin	Left in tin too long
	Too much sugar used
	Tin not greased
Cake breaks when removed from tin	Cake removed from oven before set
	Too much raising agent used
	Cake removed from tin carelessly
Speckled top crust	Air bubbles break on surface as a result of too much air having been incorporated into mixture
	Sugar not dissolved or too coarse
Cracked top crust	Mixture too stiff
	Initial oven temperature too high
Moist, sticky crust	Too much sugar used
	Mixture too runny
	Underbaked
Crisp upper crust	Too much sugar used
	Too much shortening used
	Too much raising agent used
Coarse, grainy texture	Too much raising agent used
	Insufficient creaming of ingredients
Dry and crumbly texture	Baked too long at low temperature
	Too much raising agent used
Heavy, compact texture	Ingredients too cold
	Mixture too soft
	Insufficient/flat raising agent
	Flour not folded in
Tunnels and large holes	Ingredients overmixed
	Oven temperature too high
Sunken fruit mixture	Fruit wet or damp – toss in flour to coat
	Mixture too soft to support weight of fruit
	Too much raising agent used

A

AL DENTE The Italian term describing the texture of pasta when it is cooked: tender but firm to the bite.

B

BAIN-MARIE A basting tin half-filled with hot water at 90–95 °C (about 180 °F) in which soufflés, terrines, and so on are baked.

BAKE BLIND Baking flan or tartlet cases without filling, to colour and crisp the pastry.

BAKING POWDER A raising agent consisting of an alkali and an acid. Largely, it comprises cream of tartar and bicarbonate of soda, in the proportion of 5 ml (1 tsp) cream of tartar to 2.5 ml (½ tsp) bicarbonate of soda. This is equal to 10 ml (2 tsp) of baking powder.

BEAT Mixing ingredients to introduce air, making the mixture lighter and fluffier, using a wooden spoon, hand whisk or electric mixer.

BECHAMEL A basic white sauce.

BISCUIT CUTTER A metal cutter, usually round, used for cutting shapes out of dough for making biscuits.

BLANCH Loosening skins of nuts and vegetables by plunging them first into hot water and then into cold water.

BLEND Obtaining equal distribution of ingredients by gently mixing with a spoon, beater or liquidizer.

BOUCHEE A small puff pastry case, without a lid, containing a savoury or sweet filling.

BOUQUET GARNI A small bunch of herbs (usually parsley, thyme and a bayleaf) tied together, or in a small muslin bag, and used to flavour stews, soups and casseroles.

BRAN The outer layer or husk of the cereal grain; a major source of fibre.

C

CANNELLONI Large tubes of pasta, stuffed with savoury fillings.

CARAMELIZE To cook sugar syrup or sugar until brown and syrupy.

CHOCOLATE CHIPS (MORSELS) Small bits of plain chocolate, available in 250 g (8 oz) packets, that do not melt when cooked in biscuits and cakes.

CREAMING The process of mixing fat and another solid ingredient such as sugar or flour.

CREAM OF TARTAR One of the acid components of baking powder, in which two parts are mixed with one part bicarbonate of soda.

CREAM PUFF A hollowed-out puff made from soft choux pastry, baked at high temperature, and filled with whipped cream or custard.

CREPES Thin, light pancakes.

CREPES SUZETTE Thin crepes cooked in orange sauce and flamed in brandy or liqueur.

CROISSANTS Crescent-shaped rolls.

CUP CAKES Small cakes baked in paper cases.

D

DISSOLVE To make or become liquid, especially by immersion or dispersion in a liquid.

DUMPLINGS Small balls of dough made from flour, semolina, cornflour, potato, soft cheese or even stiffly beaten egg whites. Dumplings can be steamed on top of a stew or casserole, simmered in stock or baked. Sweet dumplings are simmered in syrup.

E

ECLAIR A long, hollow finger-shaped puff made from soft choux pastry, filled with cream and usually topped with melted chocolate.

EGG WASH Beaten egg, usually diluted with water, used to produce a glazed surface on baked goods.

EXTRACT Compounds used for flavouring sweets, confectionery, and so on. They can be either natural, synthetic or blends of both.

F

FETTUCCINE Also called tagliatelle. A fairly broad ribbon noodle pasta that may be white or green (with spinach added). Usually purchased coiled into 'nest' shapes.

FILO PASTRY A paper-thin pastry made from flour and water that can conveniently be bought from supermarkets or bakeries. Each layer is brushed with melted butter before baking. Remaining sheets of filo should be covered with a damp tea-towel to prevent them drying out.

FLAKE To separate cooked food, especially fish, with two forks.

FLAN An open, round pastry case filled with fruit that is later glazed.

FLAMBE To cook food by tossing in a pan to which burning brandy or other alcohol is added.

FLAPJACK A griddle cake or crumpet.

FLORENTINES Thin biscuits made of nuts, glacé fruit and chocolate.

FOLD IN To incorporate an ingredient gently into a mixture so air is not knocked out. When making a sponge cake, folding in the flour with a large metal spoon or spatula is the gentlest way to incorporate it into the batter.

FRUIT CAKE A cake containing a large amount of dried fruits and nuts and only enough batter to bind them together. Usually no raising agent is added.

FRY Cooking in hot fat. Deep-frying involves cooking food such as doughnuts in at least 7.5 cm (3 inches) hot fat; food such as fish cakes is shallow-fried in a little oil in a shallow pan.

G

GARNISH To add decorative or tasty touches to food.

GATEAU The French word for any kind of cake. In other parts of the world the word 'gâteau' is synonymous with a rich, lightly decorated cake, often layered with liqueur, and decorated with cream, chocolate, nuts or fruit.

GENOISE Good-quality plain cake or sponge that consists of eggs, sugar, flour and melted butter that is used for filled cakes, petits fours and baked Alaska. It is baked in a flat tin.

GLAZE To impart a gloss by brushing pastry with egg and milk to give the surface a shiny, attractive appearance.

GLUTEN The protein in flour that is developed when dough is kneaded, making it elastic.

I

ICING Sugar mixtures used for coating and decorative purposes.

K

KNEAD To work dough into a mass by folding over, pressing and squeezing.

M

MARZIPAN A confection, made from almond paste, sugar and egg whites, used for modelling fruits, figures, and so on.

MERINGUE Egg whites and sugar whipped to a stiff, frothy white mass.

MOCHA A flavour made from coffee and chocolate or cocoa.

MOULD Shaping of a dough or mixture.

MOZZARELLA CHEESE A soft, unripened white Italian cheese that goes particularly well with tomatoes. This is a low-fat cheese with a compact, elastic texture that is often used as the cheese base for pizzas.

P

PASTA Paste made with flour and water and sometimes enriched with egg and oil. Used to make macaroni, spaghetti, and so on.

PASTY Small pastry pie containing meat and vegetables.

PASTRY WHEEL A metal wheel that is used for cutting pastry into various shapes.

PETITS FOURS A range of tiny sponge cakes, iced and decorated, which are served with coffee after dessert.

PIPING BAG A bag fitted with a small metal tube, through which cream, icing and other pastes are forced for the purpose of decorating dishes.

POPPY SEEDS The tiny whole grey seeds of the poppy plant used for sprinkling on bread, rolls and savoury biscuits before baking. Also used as an ingredient in cakes.

PROVE Allowing bread or cake dough to rise before baking.

R

ROUX Flour and fat cooked into a thick mixture and used as a base for many sauces.

RUB IN To combine shortening and dry ingredients by rubbing them lightly with the fingertips until the mixture resembles fine breadcrumbs.

S

SAUTE To fry food rapidly in a small amount of fat until it is evenly browned, shaking the pan to toss and turn the contents. The food is either just browned or cooked through.

SAVARIN A rich yeast cake which is baked in a ring mould and soaked in liqueur-flavoured syrup. Served cold with cream.

SEASON To add salt, pepper, spices or herbs to enhance the flavour of food.

SELF-RAISING FLOUR White flour to which sodium bicarbonate and one or more leavening acids have been added.

SESAME SEEDS The seeds of the *sesamum indicum* plant, which have a sweet, nutty flavour; used to top breads and crackers.

SCALD To heat milk to just below boiling point.

SIFT To shake dry ingredients through a sieve to remove lumps, to aerate, and to mix.

SOUFFLE A light, fluffy dish consisting of a sauce thickened with egg yolks into which stiffly beaten egg whites are folded.

STRUDEL Thin leaves of filled pastry that are rolled up and baked.

T

TUILES Wafer-thin curled biscuits served with coffee or ice-cream.

V

VOL-AU-VENT Light flaky case of puff pastry with a lid, filled with a sweet or savoury filling.

W

WASH To brush items with egg, milk or water prior to baking or to apply icing or a glaze to baked items.

WHIP Rapid aerating by beating with a whisk.

WHISK Looped wire utensil used to beat air into batters, eggs or cream.

Y

YEAST A commercial preparation containing yeast cells, used in raising dough for bread.

Z

ZEST The outer layer of citrus fruits, which contains aromatic citrus oil, and which is used as a flavouring. It is usually thinly pared with a vegetable peeler, or grated either with a zester or on a grater to separate it from the bitter white pith beneath.

Index of recipes